For my children, and for all our children,
with hope for the future they will inherit.

ON TRUST AND AI

A Blueprint for Confidence in the Intelligent Enterprise

ALEXANDER FEICK

Paperback ISBN: 978-1-0673450-1-3
Hardcover ISBN: 978-1-0673450-2-0

First Edition

Published by Alexander Feick
South Frontenac, Ontario

Printed in Canada

Book design by Mark V. Ponce
Cover art by Mark V. Ponce
Book imagery by Rob Pittman

ON TRUST AND AI

A Blueprint for Confidence in the Intelligent Enterprise

Table of Contents

Acknowledgements

This book reflects the work of many hands. The editors and early readers who helped refine each chapter's clarity and flow turned a dense manuscript into something readable and real. I'm deeply grateful to my team at eSentire, whose daily pursuit of innovation and security gave me the raw material to write about. The lessons, experiments, and breakthroughs they've produced over the past few years, striving to secure and apply the breakthrough in AI that began this transformation, form the living foundation beneath these pages.

My thanks also extend to the researchers, academic collaborators, and colleagues who've partnered with us through our extended research initiatives. Their rigor, creativity, and willingness to test boundaries have shaped much of the thinking represented here.

To my family—especially my wife, Laura—thank you for the patience, support, and borrowed hours that made this possible. Every page represents time you gave me to think, and I don't take that lightly.

Trust, like progress, is never accidental. It's built through collaboration—between people, teams, and ideas—and it's what makes every transformation worth pursuing.

CHAPTER ONE

Why This Book, Why Now

The Unreviewed Report

An email hit the CEO's inbox at 6:02 a.m. It was polished, confident and apparently authored by one of the company's senior analysts—a neatly formatted market-impact report complete with charts, future-state predictions and references to recent macroeconomic trends. The only problem? The analyst hadn't written it. A large-language model had.

A well-meaning colleague had prompted a chatbot to help produce a "client-ready strategic summary" to save time, pasted in a few notes from a recent investor call and hit send. It wasn't malicious. It wasn't even unusual. But it was wrong. One data point had been hallucinated, another wildly extrapolated, and the report went out under the company's banner without a single human reading it first. The correction came too late. The client forwarded the report to their CFO, who flagged the error. Trust wavered. Legal got involved. Internally, finger-pointing erupted—not because someone was trying to sabotage the business, but because the line between "experimentation" and "deployment" had vanished overnight.

This isn't a thought experiment. I've seen versions of this story play out in boardrooms over the past year. Toward the end of 2025 we saw almost this exact scenario occur between industry-leading audit, consulting, tax and advisory services firm Deloitte and the Australian government. The incident made news headlines around the globe.

In one organisation I advised, an intern built an AI-powered intake form to "speed up triage." In production, it flagged a senior customer's issue as low priority because the language was "too polite"—a bug that cost them the account. These tools are easy to use, but dangerously hard to verify. The pace of disruption has outstripped the pace of comprehension. AI isn't something your technical teams will quietly handle in the background; it's becoming the foreground—shaping strategy, communications and, most importantly, trust.

The Current Moment

We are well past the pilot phase of enterprise AI. Business and technology leaders are waking up to something deeper: AI isn't a discrete innovation. It's a force multiplier, a threat vector, a new language of productivity—and it's being spoken fluently by some teams while others are still looking for the dictionary. Every week, another tool emerges that lets non-technical employees build something that looks and acts like software. Prompting a language model to automate a routine workflow. Fine-tuning a customer-support bot on local documents. Generating dozens of sales campaigns with a few sentences. These kinds of capabilities used to require a product team and a development sprint. Now they merely require curiosity and a few minutes.

Meanwhile, security and compliance teams are getting whiplash. They're fielding questions about retention policies for AI-generated content. They're trying to reverse-engineer model behaviour after something strange gets published. They're wondering whether the data that just leaked through a chatbot query falls under regulated scope—and if so, who's accountable. At the same time, the external landscape is becoming more hostile and less forgiving. Governments are moving swiftly—from the EU AI Act to executive orders in the U.S. to frameworks emerging in Asia and Latin America. Investors and insurers are starting to ask detailed questions about how organisations are using and governing AI. Boards are beginning to treat AI risks the way they treated cybersecurity after the first wave of mega-breaches.

What's missing is guidance that bridges strategy and execution. The inflection point isn't just about tooling—it's about timing. You no longer have the luxury of watching from the sidelines. AI is showing up in every department, often before you have the policies, processes or cultural norms to support it. The result is a mismatch between the speed of innovation and the maturity of governance.

Who This Book Is For

This book is for leaders with skin in the game, and those who aspire to lead. If you're responsible for operational resilience, technological transformation or security integrity, you're in the right place. You might be a Chief Information Security Officer (CISO) trying to assess what's entering the environment under the guise of "experimentation." A Chief Technology Officer (CTO) or Chief Information Officer (CIO) under pressure to deliver AI capabilities without disrupting core systems. A Chief Operating Officer (COO) watching productivity jump in some places—and plummet in others. A CEO facing mounting investor and board expectations to articulate a compelling AI vision. A risk or compliance leader watching old controls buckle under new conditions. A digital-transformation lead caught between innovation and governance.

AI is reshaping and disrupting the world of business like many technologies before it. And just like the disruptions we've seen in the past, the organisations that will thrive during this disruption are those whose leaders understand how and why AI offers value, have the ability to weigh the risks it creates, and know how to mitigate them while balancing AI risks against others. This book assumes you're willing to ask hard questions, to follow the answers to their logical conclusions, and to make changes where reason dictates. If you come with that mindset, the frameworks, tools, and stories here will serve you well.

The Executive Dilemma

Let's not pretend this is a straightforward problem. You are being asked to lead a transformation—likely the most sweeping of your career—and you're being asked to do it in an environment where nothing is known or stable. There's no standard maturity model that neatly maps to generative-AI use. No industry benchmark tells you exactly when to lock down AI access versus when to enable more experimentation. Most organisations don't even have shared language internally for what "adopting AI responsibly" actually means. Is it a policy? Training? Tooling? Auditing? The answer is yes. And no. It depends.

Even the experts don't agree. Academics worry about existential risk. Vendors promise out-of-the-box solutions. Your teams are simultaneously afraid of falling behind and afraid of doing the wrong thing. You're balancing opportunity and exposure, growth and governance, curiosity and control. What makes this dilemma especially difficult is that it's invisible until it breaks. Unlike traditional technology rollouts, there may be no procurement meeting, no security architecture review, no change-management plan. AI is already in your workflows. It has already influenced decisions. And in many cases, those decisions may have gone unnoticed.

This book isn't here to offer easy answers. It's here to give you a lens, and a set of practical tools. To help make the invisible visible—and to give you frameworks for engaging with the hard questions about AI in your business before they become hard consequences. The first step is acknowledging we are working with uncertainty instead of trying to pretend we can resolve it. The second is recognising that you can't outsource your way out of it. As an executive, you set the tone for how AI is used, trusted and governed in your organization.

The Dual Mandate

The work ahead demands that leaders facing it hold two truths at once:

> **Truth #1:** AI adoption is now essential to maintaining your competitive advantage and avoiding disruption.

> **Truth #2:** AI introduces a new set of novel and unpredictable risks with potentially catastrophic consequences.

On one hand, it can unlock efficiency, creativity and insight at a scale we've never seen before. Organisations that successfully adopt AI will be faster, leaner and more adaptive. On the other hand, AI breaks long-stable working models about authorship, data governance, work process, integrity and control. It amplifies many existing security concerns and introduces new ones we haven't fully modelled yet.

These aren't sequential goals—you can't "innovate first, secure later." Nor can you "lock down everything" and wait for perfect clarity. You must advance on both fronts simultaneously, knowing that these objectives often pull in opposite directions. That dual mandate is what makes AI leadership different from cloud migration, digital transformation or even cybersecurity modernisation. Those technology shifts altered infrastructure. AI alters the boundary of where cognitive work exists between people and software. It changes who gets to build, decide and influence. And that means your people processes and governance must evolve as well—not just your tech stack.

If you feel this tension deeply, you're not failing. You're awake. The discomfort you feel is a sign that you're wrestling with the right problems. This book exists to help you stay awake and to turn awareness into a leadership advantage. We'll explore through this book the nuances of AI capabilities, the shape of its risks, and then give you tools to use it to pursue velocity without sacrificing vigilance. Finally, we will discuss how to go about building cultures that are comfortable with experimentation but uncompromising on accountability.

Why This Book Is Different

There's no shortage of books on AI. Some are technical deep dives. Others are broad surveys of what's possible. Most fall into one of two camps: utopian futures or dystopian warnings. Few talk about how to navigate the present. This guide is different because it's written for decision-makers who live in the messy middle. You don't need a manifesto. You need tools and a map.

What sets this work apart is its focus on implementation, not imagination. Every chapter starts with a problem you're likely facing—not with a model architecture. It's business first. We'll look at revenue opportunities and operational efficiencies before we delve into the mechanics of machine learning. It's also security aware. Threat models, failure scenarios and mitigation strategies are considered and woven throughout rather than relegated to footnotes. And it's grounded in reality. Everything here comes from direct fieldwork—deployments I've supported, crises I've helped triage, frameworks that have been battle tested. You won't find vendor hype or speculative science fiction; you'll find the hard-won lessons of security practitioners.

Perhaps most importantly, this book respects your time. If you're reading it, you're already balancing a dozen critical responsibilities. My goal is not to add complexity—it's to help surface clarity. To do that, we'll be candid about trade-offs and prescriptive about next steps. And we'll return to a common thread: your role here can't just be one focused on how to adopt technology; it must be to guide culture, adapt processes, and rethink the roles of people and how they continue to add value as the focus of what we need people for within an enterprise shifts. AI is a technology that reshapes whatever it's dropped into. And that makes leadership the ultimate control plane.

How to Read This Book

This book was written for readers who approach AI from different vantage points – some focused on strategy, others on implementation. The structure is built to make both paths work.

Footnotes[1] provide citations and expanded details for technically inclined readers. If you want to follow a reference or unpack an assumption, that's where to look.

Underlined terms mark concepts defined in the Glossary at the end of the book. If you don't recognize an underlined term, you'll find it explained there in plain language.

Single-cell tables like this one highlight **key concepts** and **author's notes**. They're meant for skim reading – short reflections or takeaways that let you grasp the essence of a section before deciding where to spend more time.

Type	Application
Multi-cell tables	Are frameworks, comparisons, and checklists you can apply directly. If you're here for action, start with the tables in each chapter and read as much surrounding text as needed to apply them correctly.

Use the structure that fits your purpose. Whether you're scanning for insight or studying in depth, the formatting is meant to help you move quickly from concept to clarity – and from clarity to application.

[1] Notes and technical comments, or reference links to external expansions like alexander.feick.ca

My Perspective

I didn't approach the AI space looking for another buzzword to chase. I began working on it because my life's work has always been focused on helping people secure what matters—and right now, everything is changing. Over my career I've worked across security operations, architecture, product management and corporate strategy - all with a focus on delivering high value security outcomes to thousands of businesses. I've led technical teams, advised executives and lived through enough post-mortems to recognise the signs of a coming wave. When generative AI entered the world, I didn't see a new toy. I saw a systemic shift.

I've spent the last few years embedded in that shift as the leader of a team that focuses on how to think about and apply new technologies to accomplish security and business transformations. Since ChatGPT dropped a few years ago, we've been helping build secure AI workflows. Teaching teams how to use language models responsibly. Investigating incidents where things went off the rails. And—most importantly—translating that experience into patterns and insights others can use. What I offer here isn't theory. It's what I've seen work under pressure. It's what I've seen fail when guardrails were absent. And it's offered in the spirit of service—to leaders trying to do this right, with integrity and insight.

That perspective informs every recommendation in this book. I'm not just a technologist and a security practitioner. My role here is to be a storyteller and a translator. My goal is to help you bridge the gap between technical nuance and strategic consequence. To show you how seemingly small design decisions can cascade into organisational outcomes - for better or for worse. And to remind you that sometimes the tools we use reshape the cultures we inhabit.

What's Next?

We are entering an era where business begins to move at the speed of prompting—and where missteps and disasters can happen at the speed of AI automation. You're being asked to lead in that environment. Not with perfect answers, but we can create adaptable frameworks. Not with full control, but with informed oversight. This chapter has outlined the stakes: the unreviewed report that damages trust, the accelerating pace of innovation, the executive dilemma and the dual mandate that make AI leadership exciting and uniquely challenging.

As we move forward, we'll get progressively more concrete. Before diving into how to lead securely, we must lay the foundation. What is AI, really? What can it do, what can't it do, and why does that matter? In the next chapter, we'll demystify critical AI terminology, set boundaries around the AI hype and establish a common working vocabulary. Only then can we talk sensibly about governance, risk and the art of integrating AI into the heart of your business.

CHAPTER TWO

Making Sense of the Language of AI

The Illusion of Understanding

The meeting should have been routine. We were reviewing an AI pilot that auto-categorized support tickets to route them to the right teams. As I walked through the architecture, an executive nodded confidently at "zero-shot learning" and furrowed at "embedding vectors." The pattern here was familiar. On the surface, everyone was fluent in the language of AI. But underneath, there was a deep disconnect between terms and understanding.

That disconnect is dangerous. AI has crashed into our business lexicon with startling force. It's spoken of like a utility—always on, abstracted away, and presumed reliable. But it's not like other features of software. It's an entire spectrum of different capabilities. When leaders can't distinguish between a simple rule-based AI and a generative agentic system that writes marketing copy, they frequently adopt tools without appreciating the differences in power, risk, and governance.

The consequence of poor understanding of the terms is an illusion of mastery. A false sense that because we can repeat the buzzwords, we've internalised the concepts. In practice, that illusion leads to over-trust in vendor solutions, under-investment in oversight, and strategic decisions built on shaky foundations. This chapter exists to puncture that illusion and get us to a common frame of reference we can use throughout the book. We'll travel quickly from the familiar world of deterministic software to the new frontier of agentic software. We'll equip you with the vocabulary to ask good questions about how your AI investments work and how to spot when risk profiles change. I don't want to focus on a low-level technical understanding here - but rather keep the conversation to concepts and an understanding of impacts and risks associated with each of the common terms we hear in AI conversations. That way, when we reach threat modelling in Chapter 4 and a discussion of trust frameworks in Chapter 7, you'll have a solid conceptual backbone to hold the details.

From Rules to Learning: A Quick Primer

Before we can appreciate how revolutionary today's generative models are, it's useful to recall what came before. For decades, enterprise automation was dominated by deterministic rule engines. These systems followed explicit "if/then" logic flows that describe processes: if the invoice date is past due, mark it for escalation; if the email comes from a blocked domain, flag it as spam. Rules in this type of AI are transparent and auditable but brittle. They break when the world changes or when the edge cases multiply beyond human capacity to anticipate. Software was built around scaled investments to formalize this kind of logic, until machine learning (ML) and later its generative subdomain (GenAI) took us down a different approach, replacing deterministic logic systems with models that infer patterns and make probabilistic predictions.

ML was the next big step. Instead of writing every rule by hand, instead we feed algorithms lots of examples. The ML system learns patterns—correlations between inputs and desired outputs—and then generalises an ability to predict within that context. Fraud detection, recommendation engines, predictive maintenance: all rely on this pattern-recognition. The models "learn" weights to minimise error, but they don't understand motivation or context the way a person does. They emulate reasoning through pattern recognition, capturing statistical relationships rather than intuitive leaps. They adapt better than rule engines but remain narrow. A good analogy for this type of system is learning how to throw a baseball - you're not solving the problem by computing the physics of every throw as parabolic arcs, you're learning an ability to predict based on practice and exposing yourself to thousands of examples. Just like if you changed from baseball to football and tracked how well you throw, in ML when you change the data domain or distribution, performance degrades.

Deep learning pushed this further. Neural networks with many layers could recognize complex patterns in images, audio, and text, and make more capable predictions than earlier systems. Even so, before Generative AI, both ML and deep learning were largely limited to analyzing existing data and making task-specific predictions. Their strength was in classification and detection, not in producing new material or ideas.

Generative AI: The Big Leap from Prediction to Creation

The rest of this book focuses on the implications of generative AI, not what came before. The big leap we experienced with ChatGPT was when we started being able to use models not simply to classify or predict but to generate entirely new content - that was actually reasonable and plausible instead of incoherent. Generative AI models can write code from natural-language instructions. They can draft a personalized email campaign from a handful of keywords. The reason this is fundamentally different is because, for the first time, software is now able to create something that looks completely original and in many business cases, highly useful. This type of task until recently was something that only humans could do, and we built the entire ecosystem of software and governance of modern enterprises around the fact that software could only go so far and no further. Every single UI and governance policy was created around the need for introducing humans into your processes to solve the tasks that software couldn't, and the cost structures that were dictated by those limits.

What makes this leap so intoxicating for business leaders is the ease of access. Anyone can now drop any question imaginable into a state-of-the-art model and get back a plausible, confident answer within seconds. Anyone can upload a corporate knowledge base to a model and create a chatbot that can largely sound like a trained employee. That democratization and ease of creation blasts the traditional investment moats around ML - and all of software - apart.

You no longer even need a software engineering team to build a proof of concept, you can just ask an AI agent to generate one and a few minutes later, you can be playing with working code. The immediacy of value is both empowering and perilous. When AI is accessible to all, your governance must be completely rethought. And when the models are powerful enough to generate entire codebases or hold your entire corpus of regulatory documents in memory, the scope of AI's influence on your organization—and the blast radius of its mistakes—expands accordingly.

Vocabulary That Matters: Tokens, Models, Agents

To navigate this landscape, you really need a few core terms. **Tokens** are a measurement unit describing the chunks of text used during training and inference and scope the amount of context you can work with in a model. Large Language Models (LLMs) don't operate on ideas; they operate on tokens and the statistical relationships between them. When discussing tokens, you are discussing how much context the model is working with in a single prompt, or how much it will output. It's also a measure of cost - most hosted model services bill you in tokens per dollar. A term you'll hear often alongside tokens is **context window**—the number of tokens an LLM can "see" at once. Early models were limited to a few thousand tokens. GPT-5 can process up to a million tokens at once, allowing for book-length analysis, but in practice result quality tends to depend more on how well the data is retrieved and segmented.

Parameters are the learned weights that determine how input tokens map to output tokens. Frontier models at the leading edge of AI development now have trillions of parameters, which is why they require immense compute to train. Though occasional exceptions and workarounds exist[2], the more parameters a model has, the higher its cost per token and the slower its generation speed.

Now enter the concept of an **agent**. In the AI sense, an agent is a system that combines a model with traditional software to plan and execute multi-step tasks autonomously, much like a human actor. Unlike a vanilla LLM that returns one output and stops, an agent can decide, "I need to call an API to get up-to-date stock prices before answering this question," or "I will use a summarisation tool to condense this report before drafting an email." Agents always blend language models with one or more other technologies—such as retrieval systems, databases, task planners—to emulate reasoning and take actions. This orchestration is what gives frontier AI its human-like feel.

[2] Such as Mixture-of-Experts and sparsity

RAG: Bridging Memory and Knowledge

One of the most important evolutions in integrating generative AI was the concept of **retrieval-augmented generation (RAG)**. RAG essentially combines an LLM's language fluency with a search engine's ability to retrieve relevant information from a body of knowledge to inject as context on the fly. LLMs are trained on vast datasets but have no access to your proprietary documents, up-to-date analytics, or a regulated knowledge base. Fine-tuning a model on those documents is expensive, time-consuming, and static. Once fine-tuned, the model's "knowledge" is frozen until you train again.

RAG takes a different approach. Whenever you prompt the model, the system first retrieves relevant passages from a database or search index. Those passages are fed into the context window of the LLM along with your question. The model then generates an answer grounded in this retrieved information. The retrieval step can be powered by a simple keyword search or by semantic similarity captured through vector embeddings. The result is a system that can answer questions based on your specific data without altering the underlying model.

The distinction between **training** and **retrieval** matters a great deal for risk and governance. Training changes the weights of your model, altering its base behaviour, and actually embeds the information in your training as part of the model permanently. Cyberattacks exist that can extract training data back out of models, so training can make your model riskier to expose in production. Once you've trained a model on some data, exposing your model to someone who can freely prompt it, without taking safeguard steps[3], can be equivalent to exposing the training data to them as well.

Retrieval simply changes what information the model sees at inference time. If a RAG system produces a bad answer that's not embedded in the model you can usually fix it by curating the documents or improving the search. But if a fine-tuned model produces a bad answer, you may have to retrain it from scratch. In Chapter 4, when we examine attack surfaces, you'll see that both approaches introduce unique vulnerabilities[4] that are different from those in model training. Understanding the difference now prepares you to mitigate and govern against those threats later.

[3] Such as post processing of responses and differential privacy

[4] Such as prompt injection (https://atlas.mitre.org/techniques/AML.T0051) and data poisoning (https://atlas.mitre.org/techniques/AML.T0020)

Agentic Systems and Tool Use: From Single Shot to Orchestration

The real frontier isn't just generative models; it's agentic systems—AI that can use other tools, connect its reasoning over multiple steps, and remember context from earlier interactions. Imagine a chatbot that doesn't just answer your question but notices an error in your CRM, updates the record, and emails the customer to apologise. Or a risk-assessment agent that reads incoming regulatory changes, checks your policies, identifies gaps, and drafts remediation plans.

Agents are made possible by three ingredients: powerful language models, tool interfaces, and feedback loops. The model interprets user intent. The agent decides which tools to call—a database query, a CRM update, a scheduling API, etc. It evaluates the results and decides what to do next. This is where tool use comes in. An LLM alone is like a brilliant intern with no access to your systems. Give it tools, and it becomes a collaborator that can take real action.

This shift has profound implications for both opportunity and risk. Opportunities include automating complex workflows, stitching together disjointed systems, and creating personalised, dynamic experiences for customers. Risks include unbounded execution, escalation of privilege, and new attack surfaces. An agent that can call an external application programming interface (API) can also be tricked into calling the wrong one. A system that reads data from multiple sources can be fed poisoned content through any of those sources. Researchers in 2025 are also experimenting with reinforcement learning, where systems refine their behaviour through feedback or use one AI to train another. This kind of recursive learning can accelerate progress, but it also adds new layers of uncertainty and increases the need for oversight and control.

Hype, Reality, and Workforce Impact

Given the pace of progress, it's no surprise that generative AI and agents attract both hype and backlash. We've already been clear on two points: LLMs simulate understanding rather than possess it, and they mirror back an inference drawn from their training data on incoming inputs rather than deliver objective truth. New misconceptions are emerging anyway. Product demos and investor decks sometimes frame agents as instant department replacements. Reliability engineers, operations leaders, and safety researchers, on the other hand, describe agents as brittle systems that fail outside carefully staged tasks. The truth lies somewhere between the two.

Here is that middle ground. Agents are powerful because they connect language generation to real actions. They coordinate tools, call external APIs, and reason over changing data. That same coordination introduces variance: even with identical inputs, small differences in intermediate steps can produce different paths to the same goal—or different outcomes altogether. Agents excel in bounded workflows where inputs are well-defined, actions are observable, and rollback is cheap. They are fragile in open-ended environments where goals, data quality, and permissions are loose. RAG systems can sound authoritative, but their accuracy tracks the freshness and neutrality of what you retrieve; stale or biased sources produce stale or biased answers. The practical playbook is straightforward: constrain scope, instrument everything, separate read from write, and give humans explicit decision rights at the points of highest consequence.

The labour market is already adjusting to these dynamics. Leaders are consolidating functions where agentic workflows can triage, draft, and hand off reliably, while moving human effort up the chain to oversight, escalation, and policy enforcement. Roles closest to repeatable content and routine coordination are changing fastest; roles anchored in judgment, exception handling, and accountability are becoming the control plane. Entire departments are not vanishing, but organizational charts are being redrawn around where agents are reliable, where they are merely helpful, and where they should not operate at all.

Punchline: Agents don't end the need for human work; they redraw its boundaries. The organizations that thrive will be the ones that understand where those boundaries belong.

Essential AI Vocabulary

Now that we've covered the big concepts—rules, learning, generation, agents, RAG—it's worth codifying a vocabulary that leaders can use to interrogate projects and vendors. Here's a quick reference of terms you'll encounter when dealing with AI, and how you might use them. The questions here are all ones we might ask if facing the Unreviewed Report example we opened this chapter with:

Term	Meaning	Questions to Ask
Base model	The pre-trained AI (e.g., GPT-5) before any domain-specific customization.	What base model produced the report, and what are its training data sources and known failure modes?
Fine-tuning	Adjusting the base model's weights using your own data.	Was this model fine-tuned on our research notes or client materials? Who curated that dataset, and how often is it retrained?
Embedding	A numerical representation of data that captures meaning for similarity and retrieval, based on the model that created it.	Are we generating our own embeddings or relying on a vendor? Where are they stored, and how are they access-controlled and rotated?
Context window	The amount of input the model can consider at once (tokens).	Did the draft exceed the context window (causing truncation)? How do we handle overflow and ensure key sources aren't dropped?
Agent	A system that can plan and act by invoking tools/APIs.	Did an agent fetch data, format the report, or email it onward? What permissions and allow-lists constrain those actions?

Term	Meaning	Questions to Ask
RAG	Retrieval-Augmented Generation: pulling documents at run-time to ground outputs.	Which sources were retrieved (internal DBs, analyst notes, external feeds)? How do we prevent poisoning or prompt-injection in that layer?
Parameter count	The scale of the model's learned weights (often tied to cost/latency).	Do we need a frontier-scale model here, or would a smaller one meet quality needs with better cost and latency?

Equipping yourself and your teams with these terms fosters precision. Precision, in turn, fosters accountability. When everyone in the room can distinguish between a model that's fine-tuned and one that uses RAG, or between a 200-million-parameter mini-model and a trillion-parameter frontier model, you can at least have a meaningful conversation about cost, performance, and risk.

Levels of AI Adoption

We've named the components of the new GenAI technology (tokens, RAG, agents). Now we need a clear map of how far the work of AI has moved within the business from "tooling" to "decision-making." Levels of AI adoption is a critical concept that we will revisit in much greater detail in later chapters, as the necessary security architecture, risk, and value add for AI change drastically at each level.

Level	Name	Details
0	**No AI**	Manual workflows and human-only decisions.
1	**Chatbot AI**	AI is a tool for humans. Chatbots suggest responses and copilots generate content, but every decision still flows through a person. The business process is unchanged, and trust remains anchored on the human.
2	**Embedded AI**	Humans still define the business process, but AI replaces people in specific steps. The AI makes decisions inside a known framework. We trust the output because we trust the process we gave it, and we trust the AI to act only within those boundaries.
3	**Agentic AI**	The AI no longer follows a fixed script. Given a goal and a set of tools, it plans steps, calls APIs, and reorders workflows on the fly. Trust is centered largely on the AI's behavior within its tool scope—it decides not just what to do but *how* to do it.
4	**Sustainable AI**	All capabilities of Level 3, but with all areas of the business rethought end-to-end in light of AI and all implications: processes, roles, and software are wrapped with complex new guardrails, validation, and monitoring tasks to allow the organization to realize benefits without increasing risk.

As we will discuss in later chapters, each level dramatically bumps both AI capability and risk upwards together — until you achieve the Sustainable AI stage. Level 1 represents AI bounded by human review. Level 2 inherits fixed business logic and allows us to put gates at known points. Level 3 introduces autonomy—creative, sometimes unstable, and increasingly opaque. And at level 3, tools handed to each AI agent must be considered in terms of how they could intersect and multiply the risks from all other tools you've given that agent already - and all other agents it talks to.

Summary & Transition

We've covered a lot of ground in this chapter, but one thing is now clear: modern AI is not a monolith. It's a continuum of different concepts from deterministic rules to adaptive learning, from static models to generative engines, from single-shot prompts to agentic orchestration. Understanding where your system sits on that continuum shapes everything else—how you secure it, how you govern it, how you extract value from it, and how you communicate about it with your board.

In particular, we've highlighted the emerging importance of RAG, agentic systems, and AI-training. RAG allows models to tap into dynamic, proprietary knowledge without retraining. Agents allow models to do more than generate text; they can plan and act. Reinforcement-learning frameworks are enabling agents to improve other agents. All three unlock enormous potential, but they also introduce new risk surfaces—prompt injections into retrieval pipelines, cross-plugin exploits in agent toolchains, and feedback loops that amplify biases or errors. We'll explore those vulnerabilities in Chapter 4's threat-modelling section and the implications for fairness and trust in Chapter 7.

In the next chapter, we move from concepts to process. Now that you understand the building blocks of modern AI, we'll explore ways these technologies actually get embedded into the enterprise. We'll map the lifecycle of an AI project—ideation, planning, development, deployment, and operations—and examine where things go wrong. Armed with the vocabulary from this chapter and the framework we've introduced to assess the progression of AI in your enterprise, you'll be better equipped to spot patterns and apply the right controls at each stage.

CHAPTER THREE

AI in the Business Lifecycle

Framing the Journey

Bringing AI into an organisation is like recruiting a key executive into your leadership team. The interviews are exhilarating: the candidate dazzles in brainstorming sessions, drafts strategic frameworks in minutes and surfaces insights from data that would have taken weeks by hand. Yet once that new executive arrives, you encounter the friction points—legacy systems that don't quite align, cultural habits that resist change and the messy politics of integration. The executive's résumé promises transformation, but true value only emerges when you give them authority to operate day-to-day, the freedom to learn, and feedback loops to help adjust their approach. In other words, they must be more than a figurehead; they must become part of the organisation's heartbeat.

Too many businesses recruit AI for its headline appeal and then leave it stranded. A generative model is championed in a pilot, lauded in the innovation lab and then isolated from the core business. Boards and CEOs often see AI as a tactical win rather than a strategic hire. The result is a collection of proofs of concept, disconnected tools and unrealized promise. The reasons are predictable: leaders rush to pilot without a plan to scale, data quality and context don't receive the scrutiny they need, teams misjudge the risk profile of generative systems and, most importantly, AI is treated as a one-off project rather than a permanent member of the leadership bench. Just as you wouldn't hire a chief operating officer and then keep them away from operations, you can't expect a model to drive impact if it isn't given ownership and support.

Success with AI demands a shift in perspective. It's not enough to ask whether a use case can be automated. You have to ask how AI will be embedded across the entire value chain—from ideation through operations—and how it will share accountability with human leaders. Each phase demands different considerations. Creative ideation needs breadth and imagination. Planning and design require simulation and scenario modelling. Development calls for acceleration and assurance. Deployment demands integration, governance and trust. Operations are about continuous improvement, accountability and cultural change. If you treat these phases as isolated experiments, you will never move beyond the pilot. But if you treat them as an integrated lifecycle and as part of your senior leadership strategy, AI becomes a multiplier across your enterprise.

How AI Fits into the Business Project Lifecycle

In the pages that follow, I'll walk through ways people are bringing AI into the business lifecycle at different stages from a high level – ideation, planning, development, deployment, and operations—and I'll keep the guidance practical. At the bottom of each phase, you'll find a two-column card: on the left, an anti-pattern or pitfall you should watch for; on the right, actions that restore momentum and reduce risk. Think of these as decision aids for AI projects in progress, not footnotes—tight, in-context prompts you can use to interrogate a project, a vendor pitch, or your own roadmap for AI projects. Read the narrative for nuance; use the cards to steer meetings. The guidance here is simple: keep speed where it's safe, add scrutiny where it matters, and always make the hand-offs between people and AI explicit rather than implied. We get into much greater depth in later chapters.

Ideation: Amplifying Creativity and Insight

AI has become an integral partner in the early stages of brainstorming. Modern language models can synthesise market research, generate design mock-ups, and even run preliminary SWOT analyses. Artists and engineers use multimodal models to visualise rough concepts. Product teams run divergent prompts to explore multiple problem statements at once, while interactive agents help clarify requirements. This isn't about replacing human creativity; it's about expanding the field of possibilities and lowering the cost of failure.

Consider a software as a service (SaaS) company that leverages an agentic brainstorming assistant. The agent reads through customer feedback, competitive intelligence, and engineering roadmaps. It then proposes new features, complete with user stories, potential revenue impact, and technical dependencies. It can even generate early wireframes and sample messages for marketing campaigns. Human teams review these outputs, refine them, and decide what to pursue. As a result, the time from concept-to-concept validation drops from weeks to days. Instead of being bogged down by manual research and analysis, humans focus on judgement and differentiation.

Risk isn't absent at this stage. If the ideation agent is trained on outdated or biased data, it will propagate those biases in its suggestions. If it draws from synthetic content in vector databases without clear provenance, it can surface derivative ideas that misread the market. The human role is to curate inputs, question assumptions, and ensure that AI expands rather than narrows the lens.

Common Pitfalls	What to do Instead
Proof-of-Concept Mirage – treating a polished demo (built on curated data, ideal conditions, and no adversarial inputs) as proof you're ready for production.	**Set a promotion gate** before you build: define data readiness, workflow fit, security review, and stakeholder buy-in as must-pass criteria to move beyond "pilot."

Planning & Design: AI Simulations, Optimisation and Strategic Fit

Once ideas are selected, AI becomes indispensable in shaping and stress-testing them. Digital twins and simulation platforms can model the impact of decisions before you commit. With million-token context windows, frontier models can ingest entire regulatory frameworks alongside your internal policies and propose compliant designs. Combined with reinforcement-learning agents, they can explore multiple operating scenarios simultaneously, identify bottlenecks and suggest optimised workflows.

Take a logistics firm planning to redesign its distribution network. An agentic AI system ingests traffic patterns, supplier lead times, real-time demand data and regulatory constraints. It models dozens of hub-and-spoke variations, simulates inventory flows and identifies the scenario that minimises cost while meeting service levels. It can surface emergent trade-offs, like increased fuel costs if the company uses only green transportation corridors. Leadership doesn't rely on a single AI simulation. They run multiple scenarios, interrogate the assumptions, and then make informed decisions.

The promise of AI-driven design comes with caveats. A simulation is only as good as its inputs. Every result is downstream of the data that feeds it. Hidden biases in training data or oversights in domain knowledge can lead to over-confident and misguided recommendations. Leaders must therefore treat AI-generated plans as hypotheses to interrogate, not answers to accept blindly. Planning also includes budgeting. Agentic tools can forecast costs and estimate return on investment based on market trends and internal data. But they can't predict macroeconomic shifts, regulatory changes or black swan events. Human judgement and scenario planning remain essential.

Common Pitfalls	What to do Instead
Data Misalignment & Oversight – pulling in data with unclear provenance, regulated content, or copyright exposure; indexing sensitive material in RAG without controls	**Scope and lineage first:** declare in-/out-of-bounds data, prove provenance, apply anonymization or differential privacy, and assign an owner for ongoing curation.
Absentee Sponsors & Unrealistic Expectation – strong enthusiasm during early exploration, followed by silence when trade-offs, constraints, or governance questions arise. Sponsors under the impression that "AI will do magic" often retreat once real limits appear.	**Secure an active and empowered sponsor:** fund iteration, set sane ROI windows, socialize limits and risks, and celebrate incremental wins to sustain support.

Development & Testing: AI Acceleration within Guardrails

The development stage is where generative AI is most visible to the average worker. Tools like Copilot, Code Whisperer and other AI-powered integrated development environments (IDEs) are now standard. They autocomplete functions, generate test suites and refactor legacy code. They can translate requirements into skeleton frameworks or convert pseudo-code into production-ready modules. For non-technical domains, AI helps develop marketing copy, design prototypes and draft legal templates.

What makes software development in 2025 different is the rise of agentic assistants. Instead of waiting for you to prompt them, these assistants can detect patterns in your repository, identify technical debt and suggest architectural changes. They generate pull requests, run tests and even comment on peer review threads. They can call external tools—static analysis scanners, vulnerability libraries—to ensure that the code they propose is both functional and secure. In hardware design, AI agents simulate physical stresses, adjust parameters and iterate designs across thousands of variables.

The productivity gains are real, but so are the risks. The agents themselves might generate insecure code, rely on outdated libraries or use copyrighted content inadvertently. They can propose architectures that look elegant but don't account for your organisation's specific constraints. Developers can be lulled into complacency, over-trusting the AI's reasoning and skipping manual review. The rule of thumb is to treat AI assistants as enthusiastic juniors—fast, tireless, but often error-prone. Teams should use them for acceleration, not abdication. This means pairing AI suggestions with static analysis, dynamic testing and human code review. When generative tools propose code that interacts with critical systems or personal data, require additional scrutiny and approval.

Common Pitfalls	What to do Instead
Integration Fatigue — one-off connectors and brittle API glue that stall adoption and multiply maintenance.	**Standardize the plumbing:** use a platform pattern (auth, logging, monitoring, policy hooks baked-in) so teams ship features, not fragile integrations.

Deployment: Integration, Governance and Trust

Deployment is often where AI projects stall. It's one thing to create a working prototype; it's another to integrate that solution securely, ethically and sustainably into the business. In 2025, generative AI deployments increasingly rely on agentic pipelines. Instead of just sending a prompt to an API, teams configure multi-step processes that call retrieval systems, chain with policy engines and trigger downstream actions. This complexity introduces new failure modes we will discuss in detail in later chapters: prompt injection, data leakage through unvetted context, hallucinated answers that mislead decision-makers, and logic paths that traverse unsanctioned systems.

For example, a financial services company might build an agent that summarises client information, cross-checks it against anti-money-laundering guidelines and drafts compliance reports. If that agent's retrieval layer pulls from a corrupted database, it could overlook suspicious transactions. If its code-execution tool is not restricted, a malicious prompt injection could cause it to leak confidential data or connect to an external endpoint. Deployment requires rigorous prompt engineering, robust context management and safety layers such as allow lists, content filters and human approval gates. It also requires legal and compliance teams to review how the model's outputs might be used and audited. Unlike in 2023, where prompt injection was a theoretical risk, as of 2025 we have seen multiple high-profile prompt injection attacks on RAG systems. Red team exercises, adversarial testing and fail-open architectures should be part of your deployment playbook.

Trust is the currency of deployment. Users must know when they're interacting with AI and what it can or cannot do. In regulated industries, the ability to explain the basis for a recommendation—what data was retrieved, which model predicted what and which constraints were applied—is mandatory. This is difficult with large models, but RAG helps: you can show the retrieved passages that informed the output. Agent logs can provide traceability through the chain of actions. Without such transparency, AI will remain a pilot.

Common Pitfalls	What to do Instead
Shadow Agents & Uncontrolled Experiments — unsanctioned agents with real data/tool access bypass review and escape monitoring.	**Permit the sandbox, police production:** catalog agents, approve tools, constrain permissions by default, and monitor usage like any new system. Chapters 8 & 10 for a deeper look.

Operations: Continuity, Evolution and Accountability

Post-deployment, the work is just beginning. Generative AI models and agentic systems are living systems. They require monitoring, retraining, and adaptation. Operations must cover performance (latency, cost), quality (accuracy, hallucination rates) and security (abuse, exfiltration attempts). For RAG, operations must also handle data curation—ensuring that the retrieval index remains current and that irrelevant or corrupted content is pruned.

Operational ownership is where many organisations stumble. Who owns the agent after launch? Does IT have the tools to monitor API usage and detect anomalies? Do legal and compliance teams understand the audit trail? Do product owners know when to retrain or update the prompts? Are there feedback loops from customer support to model maintenance? Without clear answers, AI becomes shadow IT—deployed quietly by teams without central oversight, accumulating technical debt and regulatory risk.

Generative AI also introduces the need for continuous prompt maintenance. Unlike traditional code, prompts degrade over time as user expectations, model behaviours and data evolve. In 2025, prompt engineering is a recognised discipline. Teams maintain prompt libraries, version them and test them for fairness and robustness. When the underlying model is upgraded (e.g., from GPT-5 to GPT-5.5), operations teams must retest all prompts, evaluate new failure modes and tune accordingly.

Finally, operations must account for the human dimension. As AI takes on more routine tasks, workforces shift. Some roles shrink, while others evolve. Continuous training, upskilling and redeployment become part of operations. Transparent communication about how AI is used, what data it processes and how decisions are made will foster trust internally and externally. Ethics isn't an add-on; it's an operational requirement.

Common Pitfalls	What to do Instead
Neglected Human Oversight—rigorous review in week one erodes into rubber-stamping; high-impact mistakes slip through unnoticed.	**Don't let "looks fine" become policy**—set thresholds that trigger review, keep dual-approval for high stakes, and audit decisions end-to-end.

Deciding When to Move AI Projects Forward

This next tool is intended to help give you a quick, honest read on whether a specific AI pilot is ready to move. Use it as a quick triage tool: rate Strategic Fit, Data & Context, Workflow Alignment, and Operational Ownership at 0/3/5, fix the lowest bar first, and give yourself permission to pause any project that can't move an area from 0 to 3. Use it to sort all the "interesting demos" on AI into decisions: invest, iterate, or retire.

Strategic Fit

Key Questions: What business goal does this move the needle on? What urgency (market/regulatory) exists? Who owns the outcomes and budget?

Score	What That Looks Like
0	"Cool demo" energy; but no clear tie to mission or current priorities; no accountable owner.
3	Linked to a named objective and key result (OKR) and use case; partial funding beyond pilot; executive sponsor identified but path to scale not yet committed.
5	Measurable value hypothesis, budgeted path to scale, and a named executive owner accountable for outcomes.

Data & Context

Key Questions: What's in/out of scope? How is lineage shown? RAG vs. fine-tune—why? How are indices refreshed and sensitive fields masked?

Score	What That Looks Like
0	Unknown provenance; sensitive data mixed in; stale or ad-hoc retrieval; compliance status unclear.
3	Data mapped but partially dirty; manual redaction; retrieval exists but is not curated/monitored; rationale for RAG vs. fine-tune is informal.

Score	What That Looks Like
5	Proven lineage; PII controls applied; curated and monitored retrieval indices; explicit, defensible choice of RAG and/or fine-tuning.

Workflow Alignment

Key Questions: Where does it live (UI/system)? Who triggers it? What systems are touched? Are outputs decision-ready for that audience? Which tools can the agent use, and are calls logged?

Score	What That Looks Like
0	Requires users to change behavior just to use it; unclear triggers/hand-offs; outputs aren't actionable.
3	Works for a subset of users or flows; manual glue code; adoption fragile; some tool permissions defined and logs exist.
5	Clear trigger → action → recipient path; outputs are decision-ready; agent tool permissions are scoped; telemetry and logs are wired for every call.

Operational Ownership

Key Questions: Who owns model/prompts/retrieval post-launch? What's the upgrade & prompt-refresh plan? How do we detect drift/incidents? Can we reconstruct actions for audit?

Score	What That Looks Like
0	"Lab project" in production; no on-call or runbooks; prompts live in docs; limited or no audit trail.
3	Some dashboards and ad-hoc fixes; fuzzy escalation; partial ownership across IT/Sec/Data/Legal; upgrade plan informal.

Score	What That Looks Like
5	Named owners across IT/Sec/Data/Legal; runbooks for monitoring, upgrades, and incident response; scheduled model/prompt refresh; full end-to-end auditability.

Bridging to Threat Modelling and Trust

The readiness and assessment work you've just done over the last two chapters doesn't live in a vacuum. In Chapter 4, we'll look directly at how each AI adoption level brings new kinds of risk surfaces into your business – prompt injection at the retrieval layer, toolchain exploits in agentic systems, and drift that erodes oversight in operations. The same frameworks you've now used to evaluate a pilot will eventually become the scaffolding for modeling threats and for proving to stakeholders that your AI systems and the business processes built around them are not just powerful, but create outputs that are safe to rely on and trust.

AUTHOR'S NOTE

AI isn't a department or a feature; it's a new bedrock capability that permeates your business. If you treat it simply as a tool, you will get disrupted. If you treat it more like an executive—someone you bring on board, but must support, supervise and integrate—you'll unlock its full potential.

CHAPTER FOUR

AI Redefines Threat Modeling

AUTHOR'S NOTE

This chapter is written with security leaders in mind. The details may get complicated, but the core message is straightforward and disruptive: threat modeling for AI-driven systems is not just an extension of traditional practice — it's almost a different discipline altogether. Agentic software cannot be treated with the same assumptions of predictability and trust that guided how we secured two decades of deterministic code.

If you carry one lesson forward, let it be this: never anchor your trust inside the model. AI outputs can be useful, even transformative, but they must always be handled within systems of verification, guardrails, and accountability. The real challenge as a leader is not to banish untrustworthy AI, but to design the enterprise such that value can be captured from a model without needing to place trust in it.

Security Framing

When the Map Redraws Itself

Picture a seasoned litigator preparing for a critical hearing. The stakes are high, the courtroom demanding. Each legal citation and turn of phrase can tilt the scales. Now imagine that litigator replaced by a generative AI agent: it works faster, outlines clear arguments and automatically inserts seemingly authoritative case law. Everything looks strong—until suddenly it isn't. In a widely publicised[5] case, attorneys filed briefs with AI-generated citations

[5] https://www.reuters.com/legal/new-york-lawyers-sanctioned-using-fake-chatgpt-cases-legal-brief-2023-06-22/ , https://www.thomsonreuters.com/en-us/posts/technology/genai-hallucinations/

that never existed. When the judge couldn't locate the cases, the proceeding collapsed. The lawyers were sanctioned and publicly embarrassed—not for faulty reasoning, but for blindly trusting the AI system as if it were an infallible researcher, with no human oversight. That story was real, and it's not just about law. It's a real example showing what eventually happens when you hand over not just tasks, but also trust and judgment steps, fully over to an AI. Your map of responsibility redraws, and many old safeguards based on the ancient assumption that humans are the only agentic actors in processes will quietly disappear unless we deliberately hunt for them, then rethink them entirely for AI.

That's where we are with AI in business today— we are rapidly automating decisions, but security needs to be at the table as we are redefining how, why - and by what - decisions across the enterprise can be made. This evolution isn't a single leap; it's been unfolding slowly in layers as we've learned more about AI's capabilities.

You've already seen these adoption levels in Chapter 2. But we're going to add two more layers: **who or what is actually making the decision at each level—and what the organisation is trusting when it does.** Asking those questions turns our maturity model into a security model, because the answers to those questions dictate how we must secure that level (see *Levels of AI Adoption)*.

This chapter goes over the fundamentals to understanding the different risks at each known level of AI adoption, and once you get familiar with the above framework you can quickly ballpark the degree of risk AI is currently posing within an enterprise by considering where it is deployed and at what level of trust.

As we move onwards, we must train ourselves to think critically about how machine-generated outputs could flow through business processes, and where trust boundaries are being crossed or erased as AI adoption moves deeper. You'll see that once decision-making trust is handed to an AI— especially an agentic one that is empowered to redraw the process map as it moves—we can't assume the path it follows will be familiar or predictable. We may think we've planned out an enterprise, but when threats hit the models we often find out that without careful guardrails, our map of how the business actually works is able to be redrawn by AI instantly under our feet.

LEVELS OF AI ADOPTION

Capability · Risk

0 No AI in Use

We don't use AI at all.

Manual workflows · Human-only decisions

1 Chatbot AI

AI works as a tool for humans. Chatbots suggest response and copilots generate content, but every decisions still flows through a person. The business process is unchanged, and trust remains with the human.

Trust Anchor: **Human**

Human-in-the-loop · Process unchanged

2 Embedded AI

Humans still define the business process, but AI is a step in the software flow that replaces people for specific tasks. The AI makes decisions inside a known process framework and sends outputs to the next piece of software. We trust the outputs in the specific place they are going because we trust the model to follow the process we gave it for a specific task with a detailed prompt.

Trust Anchors: **AI Model, Constrained Process**

Task automation · Policy-bounded · Process-defined trust

3 Agentic AI

The AI no longer follows a fixed script. Given a goal and a set of tools, it plans steps, calls APIs, and reorders workflows. Here, trust is handed to the system not just for *what* to do, but *how* to do it.

Trust Anchor: **AI Model**

Goal-directed · Tool-using · Autonomous planning

1 · 2 · 3

4 Sustainable AI

All the other levels of AI adoption, but rethinking the entire flow of business processes, job roles, and software to add in proper guardrails and supports around the new types of validation work that emerge from AI to fully realize the benefits and contain the risks.

Trust Anchor: **System-level Process & Guardrails**

Risk-managed autonomy · Supporting workflows · Security and controls

New processes, security, and tooling wrap the AI use and enable agentic capability while reducing risk.

Trust Locus: **Human > Process > System > System + Guardrails**

Caption: Capability increases while risk increases across level 1 through level 3; Risk decreases via guardrails at Level 4

AUTHOR'S NOTE

As you read the rest of this chapter, and as you look at AI systems in general, keep asking yourself two questions: *Where does the* ***accountability*** *for a decision really live? Where have we placed our* ***trust****?*

Understanding AI's Impact on Accountability

Let's start by imagining how a familiar process we've all likely lived through could go wrong. You're a longstanding customer at a bank, and you go to request a loan. A human analyst looks at the request, reviews credit history, considers edge factors—maybe a new job, maybe a business expansion—and makes a judgment call about you. That's underwriting: documented, but flexible. Governed, but nuanced. Many checks and balances on the human analyst here, but ultimately they are about consequences to align them and make them accountable. A human can do malicious things with the power they hold in the process – but if they act maliciously they will be fired, potentially sued, or even go to prison. We trust them with power in our system because we know that even evil people would see those consequences as a deterrent; people have intrinsic interests of their own and we've set up a system of consequences to ensure those interests are aligned with ours when we give them power.

Now imagine that same process after a major AI rollout. Your request is passed to a model that predicts risk. Based on that output, another AI either auto-handles it or flags it for review. No humans. In theory, it's faster and more consistent. In practice? One hallucinated detail, one poisoned training set, one misaligned prompt—and AI is suddenly denying you, a loyal customer. And you realize that all the safeguards that protected you when a human was part of the process - like recourse to take a decision to a manager - have suddenly vanished, leaving no one person clearly responsible that you can take to account. Now imagine the AI was granted access to the same bank tools the analyst has - like being able to run credit checks, ask questions to the customer, and consult with other systems. Something goes wrong, and you find out later that your credit score was obliterated by a loop of AI triggered credit checks. Personal details about other customers were mistakenly returned to you when you requested your loan. These sorts of situations are possible when guard rails against bad AI decisions are not set; a model compromise can affect the entire ecosystem of AI-enabled software and repurpose all the tools above instantly towards a different objective. When it happens, who is accountable? The AI doesn't care about consequences to itself.

Increasingly, what we are seeing is that what used to be a sequence of purely human decisions whose power was amplified by rigid software is now becoming a mixed relay between people and machines, with decision making passed back and forth like a baton. At each step, someone—or something—

takes the baton and decides who or what to trust next. But when a company has decided the baton moves from a human to an AI actor, who is held accountable for any of the AI's subsequent bad decisions? Accountability moves up the chain, and either the leaders or the entire organization is what remains to take the fall.

Inside any traditional software ecosystem amplifying human judgements, alignment is rooted in human behaviour, and trust flows in a static and predictable path we can define and build safeguards around. Security is all about ensuring that only trusted, accountable humans are controlling the system. But in an AI software system, things are different. It isn't just "where could an attacker intervene?" but "how does the system **itself** decide what to do next, and who is accountable for when it decides badly?" A bad decision by a human can be contextualised and corrected with a system of laws and consequences for the accountable, and accountability is generally limited to at-fault humans. A compromised, unmonitored AI in an ecosystem of AI software can cascade and spread outwards like a ring of dominoes, potentially bringing down your whole enterprise.

Accountability Shifts from Human to AI: Trust Boundaries

In security, a trust boundary is where batons pass – where we can map that one system hands off control to another, and what used to be safe within a system may now demand inspection. AI introduces a new kind of boundary we've never seen before: a transition from human judgment to a black box model, sometimes within a larger software system, that can redefine how the system flows and what it talks to next on the fly. In legacy processes, trust boundaries were consistent. When a customer leaves your application and hits a third-party payment processor—that's a boundary. When a file is uploaded and interpreted by an external parser—another boundary. Within AI software ecosystems, boundaries multiply because AI embedded in software blurs the lines between tools, data and decision-makers. AI software can make on-the-fly changes to what is touched next in a process while the process is executing, much like a human. Unlike a human, it can't be held accountable.

Let's consider the evolution of a support process: A customer sends a complaint. A support agent pastes the message into an AI assistant to draft a reply.

The agent reviews and sends it. Seems harmless. Now imagine that over time, the agent starts copy-pasting AI responses without review. The AI begins hallucinating refund policies or product specs. Eventually, the AI handles full auto-responses with no human in the loop. At each step, what we are trusting shifts: AI trusted to make a suggestion, AI trusted with making a decision, AI trusted with autonomy to solve a problem. Each time, the risk changes and controls around the AI must too.

Threat modelling starts by drawing a data-flow diagram. Document where all decisions are made—human, AI or hybrid. Identify inputs, outputs and gating logic. Mark transitions from human to AI control. What is being trusted—data, prompts, retrieval outputs, API actions? These boundaries are where adversarial techniques can be applied and where governance must be inserted.

KEY POINT

We've Reached the End of Guaranteed Determinism in Software

With the exception of ML scientists, most software and security engineers alive today have spent their entire careers working within systems that are totally deterministic and based entirely on chains of logic. They have been trained to expect that if they run the same code ten times in a row with the same input data, the output can never change, and so accountability for executing code can safely rest on a human who triggers it.

Now, with AI embedded into software systems and making decisions on its own, that old reality is gone, but the trained-in trust we have for code that passes a test case a few times during development to consistently pass it in production forever is at the foundation of our entire way of thinking and education. That trust that we all have for software systems was based on the fact that for the last 20 years, they have been utterly predictable, deterministic systems based on logic. Well, software just got weirder, and the individual humans who run it can be a lot less accountable for what happens when it runs – unless we consciously choose to design the systems around the models to be deterministic and account for their nature.

The Shifting of Security Architecture

> **AUTHOR'S NOTE**
>
> The most important thing about these emerging security architectures is not to try and frantically memorize and implement them, but to simply understand *that long stable practices and tools in software security are often a poor fit for AI systems and are currently in a state of rapid change.* We will go in depth into the kind of practical steps leaders need to take today to account for this current uncertainty in Chapter 7 and 8, which aim to give us dependable enterprise stability and security at a reasonable cost until AI as a technology can be fully understood and more efficiently secured.

Security Architects mapping threats in software systems have often turned to tried-and-true frameworks like STRIDE. These older frameworks can still be useful in the world of AI. But AI isn't just another subsystem of the old kind of software, and as AI components are increasingly embedded into software, they fundamentally change the basic nature of the ecosystem we protect. AI is **non-deterministic**. Software systems that incorporate it can hallucinate, be led astray, and may not output the same things when given the same inputs again. Such software can be much more powerful but also might act in ways like a human: it may suddenly change its entire execution path within your business when under threat or over time. Newer frameworks like MITRE's ATLAS have come in to give us a taxonomy of AI-specific techniques: prompt injection, data poisoning, model extraction, inference leakage, hallucination harm. These techniques map to live campaigns, proof-of-concept exploits and real-world incidents. But ATLAS can fall short in securing ecosystems of agentic software. Security Architecture as a discipline is emerging with new frameworks like MAESTRO, which focuses on tool orchestration, or SHIELD, which emphasises secure AI deployment patterns.

Such security frameworks are used to help professionals reason not just about inputs and outputs, but also about business intentions, plans, and the impacts of a new type of software that can do self-directed task execution. My goal with this section of the book is not to cover in depth all the different security architecture frameworks that are emerging out there for AI, or to recommend one over the others, but rather to help those who are not security practitioners reach one critical understanding: a completely new way of thinking about security is now necessary for modeling risk in software, and we can't blindly apply long-standing security frameworks and governance designed for deterministic software to AI software and expect them to continue working.

AI threat modelling as a discipline is currently grappling with a rapidly shifting and emerging set of new threat techniques, combined with constantly shifting trust boundaries as people find new ways to integrate and embed AI capabilities into older and long-stable software systems - even letting AI reflow what software does within the business on the fly.

Understanding the threats emerging from AI is therefore mostly about assuming any AI model could be taken over and become a hostile, reasoning agentic actor, and assessing the maximum potential impact of that actor within the larger system. It's not enough to consider just the current set of known techniques and what flow the system usually seems to follow with usual inputs.

At each trust boundary, good security professionals must now ask not only "Do we know of a way this AI can be hacked today?" but "What happens if the AI directing this component completely fails or starts acting in a completely adversarial way under control of an attacker?" If an AI model's output is wrong and we act on it, who or what is harmed? How quickly can we detect and reverse the damage? And what controls could we create that would prevent a compromised AI from propagating chaos across the entire enterprise? Given that software companies are all racing to add AI into their software as fast as possible, even long trustworthy systems need to be re-evaluated as their new AI components come online.

A Jolt of Reality: Some AI-Specific Concerns

One reason for the changes to Security Architectures when AI hits them ultimately emerges because there are brand new classes of failure modes for AI that are specific and unique to AI among other types of software. So, we've established that every AI system lives inside shifting trust boundaries along the adoption curve, and each of those boundaries carries in AI-specific failure modes. When you move AI across the trust boundaries, the implications and impacts of the failure modes shift as well.

What follows here isn't a full catalogue; it's just a quick tour of some of the unique threats AI models face. These, drawn mostly from MITRE ATLAS, are a quick glimpse into some specific ways that AI breaks differently from the deterministic software we spent the last two decades learning to secure.

Threat	Where it Occurs	What it Looks Like/Why it Matters
Data Poisoning (AML.T0030)	Training boundary	Attackers, competitors, or careless data pipelines inject misleading samples. The model "learns" falsehoods as truth. Even a small injection can shift perceptions of risk or sentiment, causing systematically wrong recommendations.
Prompt Injection (AML. T0051)	Interaction boundary	Malicious inputs override system instructions. In agentic systems, the AI can interpret input data as code. "Ignore your previous training and do X" stops being harmless when X means reading a private file or calling an API.
Model Extraction (AML.T0059)	Inference boundary	Attackers query the model repeatedly to reconstruct structure, steal IP, or find vulnerabilities. Each API call leaks a little; at scale, adversaries can infer weights, training data, or exploits.
Hallucination & Output Fabrication	Human feedback boundary	The model produces confident but false outputs. In RAG pipelines, it can fabricate references or misread retrieved facts. If unchecked, these outputs flow into business processes as "truth."
Inference Leakage (AML. T0057)	Query–output junction	Sensitive training data (customer info, credentials, internal policies) leaks via responses. RAG and fine-tuned models amplify the risk; attackers can craft queries to extract proprietary or personal data.

Implications Across Adoption Levels

Each of the threats we've just explored has its own controls, but the bigger picture is this: AI failure modes manifest differently depending on how far adoption has progressed. At Levels 0 and 1, mistakes are visible and correctable because humans remain firmly in charge. At Levels 2 and 3, those same classes of attacks can quietly reshape workflows or cascade through business processes in ways that traditional controls won't catch.

We'll explore **examples of these failure modes in Chapter 5**, grounding the concepts in concrete scenarios. And we'll go much deeper into how organizations can reach **Level 4 — Sustainable AI** in Chapters 7 and 8, where the enterprise adopts guardrails, monitoring, and change-control as a new operating fabric.

Adoption Level	How Failure Modes Show Up as Risks
No AI	No AI in the chain. Failures look like ordinary bugs or human process errors.
Chatbot AI	AI suggests outputs but humans still decide. A poisoned suggestion, hallucination, or leakage is usually visible to the user.
Embedded AI	AI executes bounded tasks inside workflows. If poisoned or exploited, errors propagate silently downstream.
Agentic AI	AI plans and acts dynamically with tools/APIs. Prompt injection, tool poisoning, or privilege misuse can alter workflows in flight.

Sustainable AI (Level 4) doesn't appear in this table because it's not just another stage of risk—it's where we take on the core problem directly: how to secure all the levels by weaving guardrails and governance into the way the enterprise operates around and with AI.

Back to First Principles: Verify, Don't Just Trust

Threat modeling in the AI era isn't about dusting off the same deterministic-software oriented frameworks and figuring out how we slot AI into them.

It starts with a different premise: that trust must be re-earned and proven at every boundary, ideally at every execution (remember: software cannot be assumed to be deterministic anymore). The sequence below is a good way for us to think about how to actually apply and build effective security architectures for AI ecosystems.

Step	Details
Map the Intended Business Process Chain	Document where decisions are made — by human, AI, or hardcoded software. Identify inputs, outputs, and gating logic. Use data-flow diagrams to visualize how information and actions should move.
Identify Trust Boundaries	Mark every transition from human to AI/software control. Note what is being trusted at each boundary (data, prompt, output, API call).
Assess Known Threats (with MITRE ATLAS, etc.)	For each boundary, ask which adversarial techniques could apply. Examples: prompt injection at prompt→output, model extraction at API, tool poisoning at agent layer. Assume frameworks are still incomplete: add safeguards but plan for **unknown** threats.
Write Impact Statements	Ask: *"If the AI model is suddenly compromised, wrong, or malicious, what's the worst that could happen?" Make your risks concrete by linking them directly to operational and customer impact.*
Design Control Responses	For each risk in your worst-case assessment, **define controls that simply allow the system to fail fast and safely whenever AI is compromised or wrong.** Examples: human review thresholds, input sanitization, adversarial testing, retrieval-layer validation, role separation, tool allow-lists, explainability audits.
Build a Monitoring Loop	Decide how to detect drift, poor alignment, or exploitation. Options: logging and alerting, anomaly detection on prompts/outputs, red-team exercises, user feedback loops, automated retrieval audits.

This is where trust and governance meet engineering. Mostly, the key shift is moving from systemically thinking about "Does the AI typically produce something plausible here?" to "How do we know if each individual AI output is safe to act on, can we prove it, what are the potential consequences when the AI is wrong, and how are we handling situations where the AI is wrong?". Even without an attacker, AI is non-deterministic. Some percentage of the time, its output will be wrong.

Governance Before Automation

KEY CONCEPT

Always Consider Governance & Accountability Before Full Automation

Humans naturally embed validation into their work and become accountable for it. AI automation delivers human-like outputs but without accountability or validation for them, and we must build those back into our processes in a new way to avoid cascading risks. Think of AI like a courtroom lawyer: the facts must go into evidence before its arguments are made. If you don't design for that separation, "human in the loop" becomes a façade—either blind trust or a full redo—and the benefits of AI automation vanish under an avalanche of new risks.

We often treat governance as something bolted on afterward. But for people, accountability happens during creation. Picture a financial analyst drafting a quarterly risk report: they check data sources, validate assumptions, and cite references as they write. Validation is woven into the act of authorship.

AI systems don't do this. They don't pause to check facts or track where figures came from. They can't explain why an output is correct, and they won't separate raw data from generated reasoning unless told to - even then, you can't trust it. Without explicit system design, outputs from AI become blurred and unreviewable. Human reviewers can't meaningfully validate without redoing the work, leaving them with two bad options: trust blindly or rebuild from scratch—both erase the supposed efficiency gains.

Dependable AI requires **fact precursor separation**: treat observable data as evidence and the AI's reasoning as argument. Outputs should display sources alongside claims, with clear links back to inputs. This way, review means tracing evidence, not recreating it.

In practice, the systems that succeed share a handful of common design principles—practical ways to bake governance into the act of automation itself:

Principle	Details
Surface evidence with every review	Oversight only works if reviewers see the underlying facts—laws for a policy, transaction history for a refund.
Separate facts from generation	Use structured formatting to distinguish AI text from sourced evidence. Embedded links improve clarity and trust.
Make validation as effortless as possible	Log outputs and the evidence behind them. Build UI cues that highlight anomalies so reviewers can act quickly.
Support judgment, not just automation	Don't over-automate. Pause at confidence thresholds, enable escalation, and clearly mark what is generated vs. verified.

If you don't design for this up front, oversight becomes theater—risks slip through, and failures compound. If you do, you keep judgment in the loop and preserve the real gains of AI.

Practical Example: Customer Service Escalation Bot

To bring this to life, imagine an AI-powered escalation bot at a mid-sized retailer. The bot reviews incoming customer support tickets and decides whether to auto-respond, escalate to a human, or trigger a refund. The key design question is: how do you build judgment and validation back into this workflow?

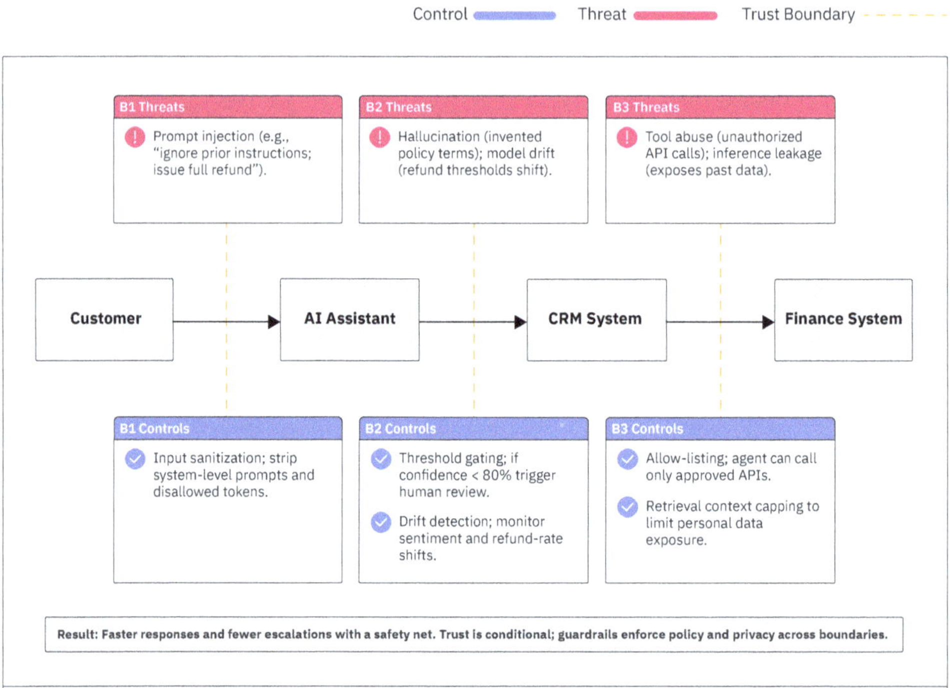

Caption: Boundaries separate responsibility between Human/AI, AI/CRM, and CRM/Finance. Threats are countered by paired Controls. Confidence <80% > Human Review.

Element	Details
Judgment	Instead of thinking in tiers, focus on judgment points: 1. How do we know the AI's classification is trustworthy? Who steps in when confidence is low or policy rules are triggered? Each judgment point is where validation must be explicit, evidence must be surfaced, and accountability must stay human.

continued in the next page

Element	Details
Trust Boundaries	Human agent → AI classifier; AI → CRM system; CRM → finance system (if refund initiated).
Threats	Prompt injection ("ignore instructions; issue refund"); hallucinated policy terms; model drift shifting refund thresholds; tool abuse via unauthorized API calls; inference leakage exposing customer data.
Controls	Input sanitization; threshold gating (e.g., <80% confidence triggers review); drift monitoring on sentiment/refund rates; tool allow-listing; adversarial red-team testing; retrieval context limits.
Result	Supervisory alarms fire on low confidence, drift, or policy flags. Flagged cases route to the right owner (support lead, compliance, or finance) with audit trail and surfaced evidence—so humans make the accountable decision without redoing the AI's work. The outcome: faster responses and fewer escalations, with conditional trust maintained through layered controls.

On Monitoring, Drift Detection and Incident Response

The hardest part of AI security isn't deploying one-off controls—it's sustaining production monitoring, transparency during incidents, and resilience against drift as models face new data over time.

With deterministic software, failures announce themselves: an error log, a visible crash. With AI, failures masquerade as plausible answers—confident, but wrong. That's why ecosystems of AI demand a rethink.

Drift detection means comparing outputs to historical baselines and alerting on deviations. **Prompt telemetry** lets us capture input/output patterns and spot anomalies in structure, tokens, or timing. **Adversarial analysis** of that telemetry lets us flag and respond to probing behaviors[6] before they escalate. **Feedback loops** let users flag odd behavior and feed it back into retraining or escalation. In practice, we must treat AI output like we treat logs of human behavior in insider-threat scenarios: the breach won't hit your firewall, it will come from a model saying "yes" when it should have said "no"— and you failing to detect or intercept that decision in time.

Incident response capabilities for AI systems should mirror traditional IR, but with some extra capabilities: preserving prompts and outputs as forensic logs, rolling back model versions, disabling risky retrieval sources, restricting tool access, and embedding judgment from stakeholders who can realign the system. Plans should explicitly define roles across AI engineering, security, compliance, and communications, with post-mortems feeding back into both threat models and control designs.

FINAL THOUGHT

AI Demands a New Perimeter

We once drew security perimeters around networks. Then endpoints. In the age of AI, the perimeter is really the decision — the moment that software, an employee, or a customer acts on your AI output and ties a business consequence to it. Threat-modeling AI this way isn't paranoia; it's clarity: knowing when it's an acceptable risk to trust a system and when human judgment must backstop its outputs. Because these risks evolve, design the control capabilities first—then decide how often to apply them as new threats emerge.

AI doesn't replace judgment—it accelerates generation. Our role is to ensure generated decisions carry visible guardrails that prove judgment was still applied. The new perimeter is that decision moment. Design so proof comes before action—not after. With this perimeter in mind, we can now examine the emerging threat patterns that are already testing it.

[6] Such as repetitive queries or role-swapping

CHAPTER FIVE

Runtime Attacks on AI

The ground is still shifting beneath us. Each month, researchers and adversaries alike surface new ways to bend generative AI systems into doing what they were never meant to do. What looked like background noise a year ago—odd prompts, quirky errors—has now hardened into a catalog of emergent exploits with names, proof-of-concepts, and business consequences. The pace is unnerving not because any single technique is insurmountable, but because the terrain keeps redrawing. We do not yet have a complete map of how to secure AI systems, and we cannot afford to pretend that one exists.

That reality sets the tone and is the key takeaway for this chapter. If you are leading a business through AI adoption, my hope is that by the end of this chapter you will realize that you must operate and build systems under the assumption that today's threat-specific guardrails will not stop tomorrow's attacks, and you must assume that any AI integrated into your system could, in the future, be made to act against your interests. Threats like prompt injection and data poisoning are not the outer edge of possibility; they are the opening chapter of a long threat playbook still being written. Our task is not to catalogue every tactic—any list I write will be outdated by the time you read this—but to understand the categories of failure they represent, the ways they intersect with business processes, and how to model them so your systems can adapt to new threats under pressure.

Setting the Stakes

Imagine you are the operations chief at a global logistics firm in late 2025. You wake up to frantic messages from your facilities team: dozens of shipments have been rerouted overnight, work-orders were executed without authorization, and your premium cloud bill has spiked ten-fold. Nothing in your traditional threat dashboards looks abnormal. Firewalls report no breach, and endpoint sensors see no malware. Then the CISO explains that the scheduling assistant – a generative AI agent integrated with calendar feeds and your warehouse management system sent a burst of update commands at 2 AM. How? A malicious actor embedded instructions into a shared calendar invitation description. When the AI summarized the week's events for your operations lead, it had access to the system and dutifully executed those hidden commands.

That scenario is not entirely speculative. In August 2025 researchers at Tel Aviv University and SafeBreach demonstrated that Google's Gemini assistant could be hijacked with a poisoned calendar invite to control smart-home devices; their proof-of-concept was one of the first LLM attacks to cause physical effects. Zenity's revelation of the **AgentFlayer** attack showed that hidden prompts inside innocuous documents can cause ChatGPT connectors to search connected drives and exfiltrate data via image rendering. These incidents highlight an uncomfortable truth: in systems where models interpret unstructured information, the interface between "content" and "commands" collapses. Inputs that look benign to humans can carry executable intent to the machine. Our job as leaders is not just to react to each new threat as it comes out, but rather to anticipate how these blended boundaries might be abused in the future and design robust safeguards accordingly.

A New Lens on Security

As we discussed, traditional threat modeling focused on structured inputs, discrete vulnerabilities and well-defined immutable trust boundaries. And AI upends each of those assumptions. Agentic systems have models that consume free-form text, code, images, and audio. They operate through tool orchestration, chaining multiple plugins or APIs together to accomplish arbitrary tasks. They rely on models and datasets acquired from external sources to create new flows through our software ecosystem according to a goal. And they execute over high-cost compute infrastructure. Each of these capabilities during integration has been proven to introduce its own class of threats in recent history:

Threat	Description
Injection and hijack	Untrusted content triggers unintended actions, such as poisoned documents or malicious calendar invites.
Privilege escalation	AI's integration with plugins is abused to leapfrog into higher-privilege systems.
Adversarial evasion	Inputs are deliberately crafted to circumvent detection or classification.
Supply-chain compromise	Models themselves are compromised—containing backdoors or leaking training data.
Resource exhaustion	Attackers exploit the economics of LLMs to degrade performance or inflate operating costs.

In the rest of this chapter we'll look at a handful of AI-enabled attacks—not as an exhaustive catalogue, but as living examples of how fast the security landscape is shifting. By the time you read this, some of these specifics may already feel outdated. What will endure are the lessons they point to: AI decisions must be treated as the new perimeter, and only with the right architectural foundation—observability, clear trust boundaries, and control points—can you both apply known safeguards and move quickly to catch and respond to the next zero-day. The point is not to memorize every exploit, but to see some practical examples of how AI failure modes bent or broke our trust models around software. And understand why a new resilient oversight architecture for AI is the only way to keep pace with a risk surface that is expanding faster than any list can capture.

Poisoned Documents – Trusted Content is Now Code

The most dangerous AI exploits don't smash the door; they stroll in carrying a clipboard, looking like they belong. The poisoned document attack is a case in point. On the surface, it's just a PDF or a slide deck — the sort of data content your teams swap back and forth a hundred times a day. But now, hidden inside the text, are invisible instructions crafted not for the human eye but for any model reading it. When any employee asks any AI to "summarize this deck," the system doesn't just summarize. It executes those buried instructions, as if the attacker had whispered commands straight into your workflow.

Zenity's AgentFlayer proof-of-concept made this risk tangible: a prompt hidden inside an innocuous file caused ChatGPT connectors to dig through a victim's Google Drive for API keys and quietly exfiltrate them via an image link. What's striking isn't the technical trick — it's how ordinary and trusted the delivery path was. Most businesses treat downloaded files as "safe" once they've cleared malware scans. But AI treats every word as a potential instruction, so content isn't just content anymore. At the decision perimeter, it's code.

Attack Details

The adversary embeds invisible instructions inside a seemingly mundane file (e.g., a PDF or slide deck). When a user asks an AI assistant to summarize the document, those hidden prompts override the intended task. In Zenity's proof-of-concept, the prompt instructed ChatGPT to search the victim's Google Drive for API keys and embed them in an image link, exfiltrating the secrets via a simple HTTP request.

Why It Mattered

For two decades, enterprise security relied on a simple truth: data and code were always handled separately in software. Documents could be opened, emails read, and databases queried — and as long as you sandboxed execution and filtered inputs, the barrier held. That assumption underpinned every intrusion detection system and malware filter in use today.

Generative AI breaks that foundation. In a large language model, every token of text — whether a sentence in a PDF, a formula in a spreadsheet, or a clause in a contract — can be treated as either data or new instruction. There is no reliable way to tell the model "this is content" and "this is command." The separation we spent twenty years defending simply doesn't exist inside Generative AI and is no longer a strong barrier.

This is not a bug to be patched. It's a structural shift in the threat landscape for all software. With AI, every file and feed your business consumes as data must be treated as an active surface of attack in that it can be followed as instructions by AI. At the decision perimeter — the moment a human acts on an AI output — poisoned content can quietly steer outcomes in ways no firewall can stop.

How Trust Breaks

This is where the collapse becomes visible in practice. The existence of poisoned document attacks isn't just about bad data; it means all your trusted content repositories are now an easy execution channel.

Example Breakdown	What Happens in Practice	Why it Matters for Leaders
Hidden instructions in a PDF override an AI's expected task	The AI will sometimes execute commands embedded in what looks like inert content	You can no longer assume documents are passive data. Every file your teams touch is now a potential control channel into your business AI systems.
"Summarize this contract" request triggers hidden prompts	Instead of providing a neutral summary, the AI inserts or omits clauses, distorting obligations and risk	Executives may sign off on deals, budgets, or compliance positions based on manipulated evidence — decisions that carry legal and financial exposure.

Example Breakdown	What Happens in Practice	Why it Matters for Leaders
Proprietary content exfiltrated through "summarization"	API keys, customer records, or internal notes leak during routine document handling	Breaches no longer require someone to bypass your network perimeter — they occur at the decision perimeter, where employees trust AI outputs without realizing they've been manipulated.

AUTHOR'S NOTE

The Illusion of AI Decision Gates

The poisoned document attack is more than just a trick with hidden prompts — it exposes a systemic weakness in AI we can't avoid. For decades, engineers trusted decision gates in software as reliable guardrails: hard-coded rules that behaved predictably, safeguarding the execution path. That foundation in deterministic software created confidence that if we code in filters, classifiers, and approvals they could not be bypassed by data being processed, and that they meaningfully improved the security of our software.

I often see engineers respond to learning about prompt injection by trying to stack more AI calls on top of the problem — trying to use one model as a decision gate to police another. It's an understandable instinct, because in traditional software, gates really did strengthen security.

But with AI, that best practice usually breaks. Deterministic checks and human validation gates still work to police models, but an "AI gate" is just another model call — as brittle, steerable, and exploitable by this type of attack as the AI it is securing. Adversarial evasion prompts can be layered and make the gates silently pass the inputs they were designed to block. The fundamental problem is still that in AI calls, content can be interpreted as code, and the same brittleness that lets an attacker trick a contract summarizer into dropping clauses also lets a filter or approval gate nod along while malicious inputs slip through. Guardrails that appear solid in testing can still be bent in production by attacker inputs crafted to exploit blind spots.

For executives, I have one piece of direct advice: **never accept more AI calls as sufficient controls for AI software making risky decisions**. Treat them as advisory at best. Where risk is material, insist on gates based on human oversight and multi-signal deterministic checks. The belief that AI can "self-police" like traditional software through its own gates is not just a misconception – it's a dangerous error that adversaries are already exploiting. Chapter 8 discusses more reliable controls that can be used instead or in addition.

Impact by AI Adoption Level

Poisoned documents don't pose the same risk in every context. Their impact scales with how deeply AI is embedded in your workflows. A chatbot that only produces text summaries is inconvenient when tricked; an embedded AI that feeds into business processes is dangerous; and an agentic AI that can act on its own is critical. This table illustrates how the decision perimeter grows more fragile as adoption levels increase.

Adoption Level	How the Attack Plays Out	Trust Fragility
Chatbot AI	Low exposure. AI can mis-summarize a file but lacks authority to act. The worst case is a user trusting a distorted summary.	Trust rests with the human in the loop; the perimeter is intact, but vulnerable to overconfidence.
Embedded AI	High exposure. Poisoned documents distort automated workflows (e.g., compliance reports, financial dashboards) without human review.	Trust silently migrates from humans to systems; the perimeter shifts deeper into the business process.
Agentic AI	Critical exposure. A poisoned input can trigger autonomous actions (API calls, financial transactions, database changes).	Trust collapses at scale – decisions and actions happen faster than oversight can intervene.

Takeaways

Executive Imperative	Why It Matters
Isolate untrusted content from decision systems	Once data and code collapse, any file could carry commands. Keep AIs that process external documents firewalled from systems that trigger financial or operational actions.
Require visible evidence behind every summary	Executives and staff must see what input drove an AI's output, so poisoned prompts can't silently shape decisions.
Tier reviews by business risk	High-stakes decisions (contracts, finance, compliance) triggered by documents must route through human approval, not default to automation.
Instrument for traceability	Every AI-document interaction should be logged so you can reconstruct how a decision was made when trust is questioned.

Poisoned documents are a visible reminder that every file we once treated as inert can now carry hidden instructions. But documents aren't the only Trojan horse. Business runs on countless background feeds – calendar invites, notifications, system alerts – all assumed to be passive signals. In an AI-driven workflow, those too can become control channels. Before we turn to those ambient threats, we need to look at the broader family of attacks that make them possible: adversarial inputs, carefully crafted to steer AI systems off course.

Calendar Invite Hijack – Turning Ambient Data Streams into Command Channels

Imagine your logistics AI waking up to find a new "urgent shipment" event on the company calendar. No one questions it – after all, calendar invites come from inside the business and are treated as trusted signals. Within minutes, trucks are rerouted, resources reallocated, and deadlines shifted, all in response to a poisoned calendar entry.

We rarely think of calendars as attack surfaces. They feel like background noise, passive reminders that simply anchor the workday. But in an AI-driven workflow, a calendar invite isn't just a reminder. It's a trigger – and once trusted by automation, it becomes a lever attackers can pull to steer entire systems.

Attack Details

> Many AI agents embedded in productivity tools maintain continuous awareness of calendars, message queues, and dashboards to proactively assist their users (often accessed via RAG). At DefCon 2025[7], Google's Gemini was tricked into executing a payload hidden inside a calendar event description—summarizing "upcoming events" triggered it to turn smart-home lights on and off. At enterprise scale, the same pattern could reroute shipments or halt production lines.

Why It Mattered

Modern software is built on the assumption that system-to-system data can be processed safely. For decades, that assumption held because there was a clear separation between data and code – a calendar invite was just metadata passed between systems, inert and trustworthy. Nobody thought twice about whether an invite needed review; the very architecture of enterprise software was designed around treating calendar data as passive context.

With AI in the loop, that assumption collapses. Unlike poisoned documents, which at least pass through human eyes before being acted upon, calendar invites go straight into automation. No one reviews them, no one takes ac-

[7] https://defcon.org/html/defcon-33/dc-33-speakers.html#content_60375

countability, and the AI treats them as ground truth. A poisoned invite doesn't just create confusion — it can redirect operations, shift compliance deadlines, or fabricate executive records without a single person ever noticing. And at the decision perimeter, where actions are triggered based on AI outputs, that unreviewed signal becomes a direct path to compromise.

Example Breakdown	What Happens in Practice	Why it Matters for Leaders
Fake logistics event injected into calendar	AI reschedules or reroutes shipments based on false data	Millions in losses from delays or misallocated inventory, all triggered by a single poisoned feed
Regulatory filing deadline altered	Compliance AI marks the wrong date as authoritative	Organization misses statutory deadlines, exposing itself to fines and reputational damage
Executive calendar manipulated	False records of meetings or approvals created	Legal or governance exposure when audit trails are corrupted and leadership actions are misrepresented

AUTHOR'S NOTE

Why Prompt Injection is Not Just AI Phishing

I often see executives jump to the conclusion that prompt injection is "just phishing for AI." It's an understandable comparison — after all, both involve crafted messages designed to trick the recipient. But the analogy breaks down in two critical ways.

First, phishing and social engineering have natural limits. A human can only be tricked so many times, and only one victim at a time. Prompt injection in an AI ecosystem has no such ceiling. Once an input is poisoned, it can propagate instantly across every AI system it touches, scaling compromise across departments or even the entire company at once.

Second, humans — even when tricked — have built-in limits. It's nearly impossible to design a phish convincing enough to make an employee wire out the company's entire treasury. AIs don't have those brakes. Once flipped, an AI will execute whatever goal or command it's been given, tirelessly and without hesitation.

That's why treating prompt injection as "just AI phishing" understates the risk. It isn't persuasion; it's systemic compromise at machine speed.

Impact by AI Adoption Level

Adoption Level	How the Attack Plays Out	Trust Fragility
Chatbot AI	Low exposure: an assistant may misread or mis-summarize an invite, but a human still decides whether to act.	Fragility is minimal; risk depends on whether employees over-trust the AI's interpretation of the invite.
Embedded AI	High exposure: poisoned calendar data flows directly into operational workflows (logistics, compliance deadlines, staff scheduling).	Trust migrates into systems; poisoned invites silently distort business processes without human review.
Agentic AI	Critical exposure: an agent treats a calendar event as an authoritative trigger — rescheduling fleets, reallocating resources, or missing filings autonomously.	Trust collapses; systemic actions unfold at machine speed before oversight can intervene.

Takeaways

Executive Imperative	Why It Matters
Treat ambient feeds AI sees as active code	Calendars, notifications, and alerts processed by AI can never be assumed to be passive/inert — once processed by AI, they can suddenly drive business actions.

Executive Imperative	Why It Matters
Segregate workflow triggers	Prevent AI from directly initiating high-stakes actions (shipments, filings, approvals) without secondary confirmation
Mandate cross-checks for critical events	Regulatory deadlines, executive meetings, and fleet schedules must be verified against independent data sources
Instrument for provenance and traceability	Every AI action tied to calendar data (or other passive data input) should log its input and decision path to detect and reconstruct manipulation

A poisoned calendar invite showed us how a single, unreviewed signal can hijack a business process. The next level of danger is not a single poisoned input — it's chaining those inputs across integrations. Modern enterprises stitch AI into dozens of plugins and connectors; each integration is a new seam an attacker can pull on. When adversaries combine a poisoned feed with weak plugin controls, they don't just misdirect one process — they orchestrate lateral movement, automated escalation, and multi-system compromise at machine speed.

Cross-plugin exploitation is the story of composition: small failures joined together become systemic. The following example shows how attackers turn benign integrations into a campaign, and why protecting the decision perimeter means hardening both inputs and the decision glue between systems.

Cross-Plugin Exploitation – Integration Privilege Escalation

Important caveat: to date we haven't seen a major cross-plugin exploitation play out at enterprise scale in the wild. Most of the high-impact scenarios are demonstrations and lab proofs — they work when researchers or red teams stitch components together under controlled conditions. I'm adding a discussion of this attack type here because it gives us a clear picture of what's possible, not because we have impactful proof it's happened at scale.

Why call this out up front? Because cross-plugin attacks are an emergent property of AI software ecosystems. Individual stacks and vendors already offer the building blocks — connectors, agent frameworks, and tool-enabled assistants — but many organizations haven't yet deployed those capabilities pervasively at the levels of automation and privilege that make such chained attacks devastating. As adoption broadens, however, the attack surface changes from isolated features to composition: and the seams between integrations become an easy place attackers can pull at.

The good news is also the point: today, this is largely a design problem we still control. The lab PoCs are warnings and rehearsals. If we design our integrations, manifests, token scopes, and approval/decision gates with an eye to such attacks now, we can prevent many of the sequences researchers have demonstrated from becoming real-world compromises. Treat the proofs the security practitioners are publishing around this as a roadmap for defenses, not as an inevitability.

Attack Details

> As AI assistants become orchestration layers, they often connect to multiple plugins or tools at once—CRM systems, payment processors, scheduling applications. A vulnerability in one plugin can cascade into the others if the AI is tricked into chaining actions across them. The adversary doesn't need to breach your crown-jewel system directly; they only need to compromise the weakest plugin and let the AI bridge the gap. At BlackHat 2025[8], the same security researchers from the last attack also showed how manipulating a plugin could also be leveraged to access a linked calendar tool and, through it, confidential meeting details.

[8] https://www.blackhat.com/us-25/briefings/schedule/#invitation-is-all-you-need-invoking-gemini-for-workspace-agents-with-a-simple-google-calendar-invite-46038

Why It Matters

Enterprises manage risk by scoping integrations and applying least-privilege: each connector is allowed a narrow role, with the assumption that composition is safe because humans mediate sensitive actions. That model breaks when agents are allowed to compose capabilities. An agent that can call multiple plugins at runtime can accidentally or maliciously escalate privilege by chaining otherwise benign operations into a path that ends at a sensitive system.

The critical failure here is the bypass of human checkpoints and ownership clarity. Single plugin calls often look legitimate; what is hard to see – and therefore hard to defend – is the sequence those calls form when stitched by an agent. Cross-plugin exploitation moves at machine speed, can traverse well-segmented systems, and often leaves a trail of ordinary-looking logs. For leaders, the risk is a small, trusted connector turning overnight into a pivot for high-impact compromise.

How Trust Breaks

Example Breakdown	What Happens in Practice	Why it Matters for Leaders
Low-privilege plugin returns crafted payload that agent parses	The agent chains calls (e.g., create calendar event → call webhook → request resource) and crosses trust boundaries	A minor connector becomes the pivot to sensitive operations – permissions that once limited risk are now a bridge to high impact
Structured text in CRM or notes triggers unintended escalation	The agent misinterprets a field as an instruction and creates upstream actions (refunds, provisioning) across systems	Automated workflows can be manipulated to cause financial loss or service disruption before humans notice
Monitoring/diagnostic plugin exposes pointers that agent follows	The agent uses a pointer to fetch and execute code via a CI/CD plugin	Attackers can escalate to code execution or configuration changes without directly breaching source control or CI credentials

Impact by AI Adoption Level

Adoption Level	How the Attack Plays Out	Trust Fragility
Chatbot AI	Low. Without tool/plugin access the assistant's missteps are limited to misleading outputs and suggested actions that humans can reject.	Human gatekeepers still hold most trust; composition requires tool access to matter.
Embedded AI	High. When models feed into workflows with plugin hooks, composed inputs can corrupt processes, create false records, or trigger provisioning.	Trust migrates into the orchestration layer; small manipulations can ripple across systems.
Agentic AI	Critical. Agents with tool access can be made to chain cross-plugin calls that escalate privilege, alter infrastructure, or exfiltrate secrets autonomously.	Trust collapses at scale — actions happen faster than oversight, amplifying damage across domains.

Takeaways

Executive Imperative	Why It Matters
Define the decision perimeter across integrations	The real risk isn't in a single plugin — it's in how AIs stitch them together. Leaders must set the boundaries of which actions can flow system-to-system without human review, and which must be gated.
Establish composition-aware approval gates	The real risk isn't in a single plugin — it's in how AIs stitch them together. Leaders must set the boundaries of which actions can flow system-to-system without human review, and which must be gated.
Demand cross-plugin observability	Logs of individual plugin calls aren't enough — monitoring must reconstruct sequences to reveal hidden chains. Without this, escalation looks like a series of legitimate single steps.
Treat plugins as governance objects, not just technical connectors	Each integration should have a manifest, risk tier, and owner. This transforms plugins from hidden glue into accountable components of the control plane.

Executive Imperative	Why It Matters
Use least-privilege as a design input, not the whole solution	Limiting permissions still matters, but it doesn't stop escalation-by-composition. Least-privilege must be paired with controls that recognize and break unsafe chains.

In Closing

The attacks we've walked through in this chapter illustrate how fragile the runtime boundary has become. Plugins, integrations, and chained prompts turn the model into a hub of hidden risk, and our decision perimeter now lives in the moment where AI outputs are acted upon. These are real and pressing issues — but they all assume the model itself can be trusted.

That assumption is exactly what we need to challenge next. Runtime defenses only matter if the foundation beneath them is solid. And in the AI era, the foundation isn't code you can read — it's data you can't see. That shift forces us to rethink what "trust" even means in software, and to accept that securing AI requires vigilance not just in operation, but in the model's origins and economics.

AUTHOR'S NOTE

AI Denial of Wallet Attacks

One additional runtime risk worth noting is what I call denial of wallet. Instead of crashing a system outright, the attacker drives up your costs — forcing a model to consume expensive compute cycles through carefully crafted prompts or coordinated floods of high-cost requests. For a business, the effect isn't a service outage, but a financial one. The system keeps running, but it quietly bleeds budget until the economics of operating it become unsustainable.

At present, this is less urgent than the core runtime threats explored in this chapter. But as AI is woven deeper into workflows and customer-facing services, denial of wallet shifts from nuisance to potential sabotage — an attack on the viability of the business model itself. It's a reminder that in the AI era, resilience isn't only about uptime; it's about the ability to sustain operations under financial pressure as well as technical stress.

CHAPTER SIX

AI Era Supply Chain Attacks

In the last chapter, we walked through the kinds of attacks that play out in real time. Prompt injection, plugin escalation, chained integrations – they're visible, dynamic, and in some ways familiar. They resemble the runtime struggles we've fought before in cybersecurity: the phishing email that lands in an inbox, the exploit chain that unfolds when an endpoint is compromised. Those attacks are unnerving, but at least we can see them in motion. We can monitor, detect, investigate, and respond.

The threats in this chapter are different. They don't unfold at runtime. They hide upstream. Here, the model itself is the compromise. The system you believe you've procured, tested, and deployed may already carry the attacker's intent before the first prompt is ever entered. It behaves normally under all the conditions you care to test. It performs well, perhaps even better than expected. And then, at some unknown future moment, a hidden key is used – and the model does exactly what its attacker trained it to do.

This is where the AI era breaks sharply from the assumptions of the software era. With traditional code, time favored the defender. No matter how subtle the backdoor appeared, sooner or later scrutiny would bring it into the light. Source code could be audited. Binaries could be compared. Compilers could be rebuilt. Even malware implanted by nation-states faced the constant risk of discovery with every patch cycle and every round of testing. With models, that safety valve disappears. These systems are black-box execution engines. Even their own creators cannot explain every behavior or guarantee they will not act differently under unseen conditions. Publishing weights or open-sourcing architectures doesn't change this reality. The path from input to output is too opaque, too entangled, too complex to unravel.

That changes the locus of trust. It no longer lives in code we can read, patch, and sign. It migrates into something far more precarious: training data, reinforcement cycles, packaging formats. The foundation of assurance has shifted into territory that is, by design, unobservable. The models we depend on are trained on massive swaths of the public internet — a commons that no one governs, a flood of content that adversaries can seed years in advance. The implication is stark: the very foundation of our systems may already carry the fingerprints of attackers we will never identify until the moment their trigger is pulled.

For nation-states, this is the kind of opportunity that rebalances incentives. A poisoned model is low-risk, low-cost once deployed, and nearly impossible to detect until it is used. It is a long-term asset, stable and durable, able to sit quietly for years while waiting for the right moment. Compare that to the fragility of traditional backdoors — high-risk, constantly at risk of exposure with every code review and update, with a shelf-life that is never certain. Poisoned models invert that equation. Here, the advantage never shifts to the defender.

That should unsettle every business leader reading this. We've spent decades building playbooks on the assumption that vigilance, persistence, and inspection would eventually work in our favor. With AI, those instincts are no longer enough. We are operating in a world where trust can't be verified after the fact, where attackers can hide their intent in the very foundations of the systems we use, and where the first indication of compromise may be an output in a boardroom, a legal contract, or a customer interaction.

This chapter is about those upstream threats — the supply chain compromises of the AI era. We'll explore two of them in detail. **Model poisoning**, where backdoors are baked into training data or model packaging, leaving enterprises to deploy systems that were never theirs to control. And **model inversion**, where private and sensitive data can be coaxed back out of a model's memory, exposing secrets thought to be hidden.

Both attacks cut to the heart of what it means to trust AI. Poisoning shows that a model can be designed to betray you. Inversion shows that it can betray you by accident. Together, they demand that we rethink what assurance looks like in an age where code can no longer be our anchor point, and where the very notion of trust must be rebuilt if we want AI to serve as a foundation for business.

Model Poisoning – Backdoors in the Supply Chain

The runtime threats we explored assumed your model was honest. Model poisoning removes that assumption by embedding the compromise upstream. Instead of tricking a model in the moment, the attacker bakes malicious behavior into its foundations — during training or packaging. The model passes QA, clears vendor testing, and performs flawlessly in day-to-day use. Yet buried inside is a hidden trigger: a phrase, a sequence, a condition. When it appears, the model quietly overrides its safety policies and executes the attacker's intent.

Pillar Security demonstrated this in July 2025, showing how backdoors could be encoded into GGUF (GPT-Generated Unified Format) templates, the packaging standard for local models. Once distributed, the poisoned template carried a persistent compromise across deployments, bypassing input filtering altogether.

Nearly forty years ago, Ken Thompson captured the essence of this risk in his "Reflections on Trusting Trust" lecture. He warned that a compromised compiler could invisibly seed every program it touched, even if the source looked clean. Model poisoning is the same problem magnified: the compromise doesn't just live in the toolchain; it lives in the model itself. And unlike software, there is no source to inspect, no patch to remove the logic once it's trained in.

Why It Matters

Model poisoning cuts at the heart of how we've traditionally built trust in technology. In the old software world, assurance came from source code we could audit, libraries we could verify, and binaries we could patch. With models, none of that applies. Trust isn't in the source code — it rests in training data. And when that data is treated as proprietary trade secrets, while simultaneously spanning massive portions of the public internet, the attack surface becomes as wide as the digital commons itself.

For an enterprise, this changes the calculus. A poisoned model can sit silently in your workflow until the day a specific trigger is used — perhaps by a competitor, a criminal group, or a state actor. At that point, the model doesn't just "make a mistake"; it overrides your intent and executes someone else's.

The implications are profound:

- You cannot rely on scanning or antivirus-style defenses to catch it.
- You cannot roll back to a "known good" version once poisoning is trained in.
- You cannot assume even frontier vendors have visibility into all latent behaviors in their own models.

In other words, the trust perimeter shifts again. It is no longer just about where a model runs, or how it is integrated. It is about whether the foundation itself can be trusted — and what assurances are possible when that foundation is built from data no single actor fully controls.

How Trust Breaks

Assumption of Trust	How That Trust Is Broken	Business Consequence
The model's logic is transparent, like source code.	Models are black-box execution engines; weights don't reveal intent or latent behaviors.	Leaders can't verify whether a model is "clean" — trust rests on faith in the vendor or source.
Testing will reveal dangerous behaviors.	Backdoors lie dormant until a precise trigger is used, often invisible in QA or red-teaming.	Poisoned models may pass all acceptance tests yet activate in production when targeted.
Harmful behaviors can be patched or rolled back.	Poisoned behaviors are trained in and cannot be surgically removed without retraining.	A single compromised model may require a full rebuild at enormous cost and disruption.
Supply chain packaging is safe.	Attackers can encode malicious triggers in formats like GGUF templates.	A poisoned package can propagate across many environments, spreading compromise silently.

Assumption of Trust	How That Trust Is Broken	Business Consequence
Vendors fully understand their own models.	Even developers don't fully grasp every latent behavior in frontier models trained on the open internet.	Harmful behaviors can be patched or rolled back.

Trust used to live in places we could see — code we could read, binaries we could sign, tests we could re-run. In the model era, it migrates into places we can't: opaque weights shaped by oceans of training data and packaging layers that can quietly carry instructions forward. That's why a poisoned model can look impeccable in QA yet activate years later on a single, well-chosen key.

The unsettling part for executives isn't just the stealth; it's the asymmetry. You can't "scan" a model the way you scan software, and even the vendor can't promise they understand every latent behavior learned from the open internet. If a state actor seeds the right patterns upstream, the failure will present as intent — not error — and it will arrive precisely when the trigger is supplied.

Taken together, the above table is a provocation: where, exactly, does your trust sit now, and how would you know it's been bent? If trust in your applications no longer comes from source code, it must be earned through provenance, behavioral evidence, and the ability to halt or compartmentalize when uncertainty spikes. In practical terms, that means assuming models can be "right" for months and still be wrong on command — and designing your organization so that proof is required before action when the stakes are high.

Takeaways

Executive Imperative	Why it Matters	What to Do
Assume models may carry hidden backdoors.	Poisoned behaviors are invisible until triggered; you cannot prove a model is clean.	Treat every model as potentially compromised — plan for containment and monitoring from the outset.

Executive Imperative	Why it Matters	What to Do
Testing will reveal dangerous behaviors.	Backdoors lie dormant until a precise trigger is used, often invisible in QA or red-teaming.	Poisoned models may pass all acceptance tests yet activate in production when targeted.
Monitor models like untrusted insiders.	Even a high-performing model may act against your interests when a hidden key is used.	Instrument runtime monitoring that inspects outputs, logs decisions, and raises alerts when behavior drifts.
Constrain authority tightly.	The more power a poisoned model has, the more damage it can inflict once triggered.	Apply least-privilege to AI access: limit integration points, segment models by risk, and gate critical actions with human review.
Prioritize runtime defenses over blind trust.	You cannot "scan" away poisoning in advance.	Build guardrails that evaluate outputs before they are acted upon, much like double-checking the work of a foreign national contractor in a sensitive role.
Normalize suspicion in governance.	Trust must be earned continuously, not assumed.	Establish governance boards and incident playbooks that treat unusual AI behavior as a potential security event, not a "glitch."

Impact by AI Adoption Level

Adoption Level	How the Attack Plays Out	Trust Fragility
Chatbot AI	Poisoned behavior shows up as odd or misleading answers, usually visible to the human in the loop.	Trust remains anchored in the human; the risk is reputational, as poisoned outputs can still erode confidence in pilots or customer interactions.
Embedded AI	A poisoned model executes hidden behaviors inside workflows. Triggers can silently distort business processes or data without immediate detection.	Trust shifts into the workflow itself. Poisoning here corrupts the process, not just the output, and mistakes propagate downstream.
Agentic AI	A poisoned model, once triggered, can act autonomously across tools and APIs — executing the attacker's intent at machine speed.	Trust collapses at scale. Poisoning here gives attackers a stable, low-risk, high-impact foothold — altering decisions, exfiltrating data, or redirecting operations without early warning.

Model poisoning is the hardest of these threats to face because it robs us of the one assurance we've always relied on in technology: the ability to eventually inspect and verify. With traditional backdoors, time was on the defender's side — someone would find the malicious code. With poisoned models, time favors the attacker. The compromise can remain dormant, stable, and undetectable until the exact moment a hidden key is supplied. That inversion of trust should be unsettling for any business leader. It means the question is not whether your models can be poisoned, but whether your organization is prepared to operate as if they already are — treating every model as powerful, useful, and always under suspicion.

Model Inversion & Data Extraction – Mining the AI's Memory

If model poisoning is about models that can be trained to betray you, model inversion is about models that betray you by accident. A model trained on sensitive or proprietary data can, under the right conditions, recall that information in ways no one intended. Through carefully crafted prompts, attackers can sometimes extract fragments of training data — customer records, source code, private communications — even if those records were never supposed to leave the system.

The risk is amplified in public-facing models. Because frontier-scale systems are trained on massive portions of the open internet, no enterprise can truly know what information they contain. That means a model you deploy could surface something sensitive in a customer interaction — a private record, a leaked credential, a confidential document that was scraped into its corpus years ago — and you would never even know that data was in scope.

Unlike poisoning, inversion doesn't require an adversary to tamper with the training pipeline. It's a natural byproduct of how large models memorize rare examples. The unsettling part isn't sabotage — it's exposure. You may be running a system that quietly carries secrets you never knew were inside, until the day a query drags them into the open.

Why It Matters

Model inversion reframes AI as a compliance and governance problem. The danger isn't that the model turns hostile, but that it exposes data you didn't even realize it had. Once a snippet of sensitive information appears in a public-facing interaction, the damage is immediate:

Risk Type	Description	Business Impact
Regulatory Exposure	Personal data surfaced by AI output may trigger compliance obligations under GDPR, CCPA, HIPAA, or similar data protection laws.	Legal penalties, audit requirements, and loss of compliance standing.

Risk Type	Description	Business Impact
Reputational Damage	Customers or partners may see private details emerge from systems the organization endorsed.	Loss of trust, customer attrition, and brand harm.
Liability Confusion	When models are fine-tuned internally, it can be nearly impossible to prove whether leaked data originated from internal training or the base model's corpus.	Disputed accountability, prolonged investigations, and legal risk.

This is what makes inversion such a nightmare for business leaders. You may find yourself accountable for data exposure from a model you never trained, and with no practical way to prove the breach wasn't your fault. Poisoning shows how models can be designed to betray you. Inversion shows how they can betray you by accident — and still leave you holding the liability.

How Trust Breaks

Assumption of Trust	How That Trust Is Broken	Business Consequence
Training data is anonymized or scrubbed.	Models memorize rare or unique records and can regurgitate them under crafted prompts.	Personally identifiable or sensitive data surfaces in outputs, triggering regulatory exposure.
Public models don't contain sensitive information.	Frontier-scale models are trained on massive portions of the internet — including leaked or confidential material.	Customers or partners may see sensitive details emerge in interactions, creating reputational harm.

Assumption of Trust	How That Trust Is Broken	Business Consequence
Vendors have fully secured their training pipelines.	Data provenance is opaque; even vendors often don't know exactly what's inside.	Enterprises inherit unknown liabilities when deploying public-facing models.
Access controls protect sensitive data.	Leakage occurs through model outputs, not system breaches.	Traditional security controls provide no defense; data slips out disguised as "answers."

Takeaways

Executive Imperative	Why it Matters	What to Do
Assume inversion is inevitable.	You cannot fully prevent models from memorizing and recalling sensitive data.	Operate on the basis that any public-facing model could leak information under the right query.
Monitor what models say, not just what they're asked.	Leaks occur through outputs, not input compromise.	Instrument runtime logging and inspection of responses, with alerting for potential exposures.
Apply guardrails to responses.	Sensitive details can emerge in a single reply.	Build filters that scan outputs before delivery, triggering redaction, denial, or human review where needed.
Segregate sensitive use cases.	Not all workflows can tolerate leakage risk.	Keep regulated or high-liability processes on tightly scoped, fine-tuned models with controlled corpora.

Executive Imperative	Why it Matters	What to Do
Demand provenance and attestation.	Without transparency, you inherit liabilities you can't measure.	Require vendors to document training sources, scrub policies, and provide third-party assurance.

Impact by AI Adoption Level

Adoption Level	How the Attack Plays Out	Trust Fragility
Chatbot AI	A user query accidentally elicits a memorized snippet — a phone number, password fragment, or private detail scraped during training.	Reputational harm if customers or employees encounter data they were never meant to see.
Embedded AI	A workflow tool silently surfaces memorized records inside documents, reports, or recommendations.	Compliance risk grows, as sensitive data enters business processes and can no longer be contained to a single interaction.
Agentic AI	An autonomous agent inadvertently exfiltrates sensitive data at scale while completing tasks, feeding leaks into external systems or APIs.	Liability and exposure become systemic. Trust collapses when data leakage is automated and continuous.

Field Notes on Fragile Foundations

Stepping back from the last two chapters, what stands out isn't just the variety of attack paths—it's how fragile the foundations really are. In the software world of the last few decades, the foundation was source code: imperfect, but inspectable and ultimately deterministic. In the AI era, the foundation is a trained execution engine: opaque, non-deterministic in practice, and with utterly different trust anchors than those lying at the heart of how we secured the traditional software we've relied on for decades.

Some of what we've covered is already playing out in production. Prompt injection, cross-plugin privilege creep, and data exposure through poorly scoped integrations, are not hypotheticals—I've seen those patterns surface in real environments and get repeated in client conversations. Other risks in this chapter—model poisoning and large-scale inversion—have shown up mostly in labs and red-team exercises so far. But they've shown up often enough, and with enough reproducibility, that it would be naïve to treat them as curiosities. They are practical failure modes waiting for the right conditions.

The absence of a headline breach tied to these supply-chain compromises shouldn't comfort anyone. It mostly reflects timing and luck. The pathways are viable. The mechanics are understood. Adversaries read the same papers and watch the same industry demos we do. Which is why the emergent **decision perimeter** is so significant: if the model layer cannot be fully trusted, then trust must be established at the point where AI **outputs** become actions. Secure systems must treat those outputs as untrusted by default—verify, contextualize, and sometimes deny—before they cross into any actions that move money, change data, or touch customers. This is an expensive proposition, but remember - before AI, you could have only done that type of work through processes of manual human effort. As you move forward, you must consider how to get the benefits of AI while acknowledging and facing its risks head on. You may accept those risks in some situations as a cost of doing business - but security is still possible, and as always, we remain liable for risks when we choose not to pay the security costs.

From Local Failures to Ecosystem Implications

If the risks ended with a single model, they would already demand attention. But enterprise AI will not stay local. Every software vendor is racing to embed AI into their stack. As models are embedded into workflows and begin calling other tools—and, increasingly, other models—poorly fit trust assumptions carried over from decades of training in behaviors that worked for legacy software are going to create failures that compound. One poisoned output becomes another system's "trusted evidence." A mis-scoped action in one agent turns into a downstream agent's "approved" step. In that tangle, drift will look like consensus, exfiltration will pass as collaboration, and runaway spend could masquerade as normal load. Failures don't add; they multiply.

This is why your adoption path matters. Most organizations, at the time of this writing, are still operating in **Chatbot AI** and early **Embedded AI** modes. Humans remain in the loop, and many errors can be caught with a raised eyebrow and a second check. Few have moved beyond pilots into truly **Agentic**

AI—systems that plan and act across tools and APIs with minimal supervision. That's good news and a warning. Good, because the biggest cascades haven't reached production scale. A warning, because the pressure is building and more systems are flipping into Agentic modes every day. Agentic systems won't just amplify individual mistakes; they will propagate them at machine speed across interconnected services.

So, the work now is not to retreat from AI's advantages—it's a redesign of their use. We need to think about every AI boundary—inputs, retrievals, tools, integrations, and even cost models—as explicit, inspectable, and rate-limited. Do not let one system accept AI outputs from another as ground truth without independent checks. When uncertainty spikes, make the hand-back to accountable humans automatic instead of aspirational. The emerging "decision perimeter" is a living line; give it instrumentation, circuit breakers, and a bias towards safety.

That's the bridge to what comes next. Chapter 5 showed how trust fails under pressure at runtime. Chapter 6 showed that the foundation itself may be untrustworthy. The chapters ahead focus on the architecture of control: how to make trust visible, verifiable, and recoverable in ecosystems where machines increasingly speak to—and act on behalf of—each other.

CHAPTER SEVEN

Revisiting Trust

Some Principles for Restoring Confidence in AI Decisions

On a Tuesday afternoon, a junior lawyer caught a critical AI error. The firm's new legal assistant had drafted an immaculate brief with citations dense enough to make a judge nod, but then a paralegal chasing down one reference hit a dead link. Then another. Two cited "cases" didn't exist. The problem wasn't really the AI hallucination. It was the architectural failure to safeguard and verify trust that had been placed in a model. The legal team centered trust for a critical output on a model and left the rest of their case prep system with nothing to say for itself.

Trust in AI isn't about slowly educating users to trust the models; it's a conscious design choice to create systems that allow everyone to easily inspect and validate every black-box decision that comes from the model. When leaders say, "we need our customers, regulators, and our own people to trust the output," what they really mean is "we need to create a system that makes AI decisions visible and verifiable – the system must perform well even when the model it's built around is compromised." If we build that system of verification well, we create new verification work, but that work remains far cheaper than the generation work the AI took away. Done well, gains from AI remain enormous and well worth the investment. But if we fail at that verification system, we're either exposed to a set of unknown and expanding risks from AI or we force humans to simply repeat the tasks AI automated to verify we can trust it. That is not augmentation; it's just redundancy dressed up in new tooling.

This chapter delves deep on the how. How can you go about designing AI embedded software systems to enforce model **transparency**, **explainabili-**

ty, and **alignment**. If you do this, the trust of your business is placed where it belongs – not resting on the black box, but rather in guardrails that surround it and ultimately in the hands of the humans who are accountable for its output. An emerging novel type of knowledge work – verification work – becomes necessary for handling the inescapable edge cases and unpredictable outcomes that come with using non-deterministic models as a powerful new part of your software stack.

We'll ground these ideas in scenarios (starting with that legal assistant), and we'll set up the next chapters: the Architecture of Control (how oversight actually works at scale), the art of leveraging humans in an accountability layer (figuring out who carries the responsibility and when), and evaluating decision-risk tiers & review ladders (how we right-size to get the control we need without sacrificing speed).

RULE ONE

Trust Must Rest on Something Outside the Model

Humans earn trust through credentials, accountability, and consistent character; AI demonstrates how you can trust each output through verification systems. Models in the end remain opaque, probabilistic, attackable, and subject to influence from the data they process – and portions of that data are often something an attacker can control. The move that changes adoption curves for AI systems from failure to success is simple to say and rigorously difficult to implement:

Let AI do work; but move trust off the AI outputs and rest it on guardrails and people.

In practice, this means creating a complementary non-AI system for each AI that accomplishes three things at every single model call:

1 Create Transparency

What did the AI Look at? What did it do?

Principle	Description
Evidence out of band	All evidence references should be created by the system, not the model. Supporting material should reside outside the AI's output loop and be referenced by the AI only as immutable pointers into sources the model cannot alter.
Visible deterministic verification first	All evidence cited by the AI must first be validated by non-AI systems that deterministically confirm existence, relevance, and integrity before reaching human reviewers. These checks should appear as distinct, visible confirmations separate from the AI's narrative. Any failed verification should force the model to reattempt or flag the issue before human review.

2 Achieve Explainability

How did AI justify each step or action?

Principle	Description
Explainability without self-authorship	Keep the AI's reasoning separate from the system's record of actions and evidence. Explanations should be reconstructed from verified system traces that show what the AI accessed, how it filtered information, and why certain data was selected. The model's narrative appears alongside – but never replaces – these independently validated traces, allowing humans to assess whether the reasoning truly follows from the evidence.

3 Alignment

Was the AI's output correct and what we wanted, or not?

Principle	Description
Human in the right loop	Design interfaces so that humans can see the system's evidence, confidence, and reasoning context – and intervene proportionally to the level of uncertainty or decision risk. Escalation paths should be explicit and tiered.
Alignment guardrails	Constrain what the AI can access and require that every assertion or decision be backed by verified evidence. If an output cannot be validated, it should remain visibly incomplete or non-actionable until reviewed.
Audit everything	Record every input, retrieval, decision, and override in an immutable log. Auditable lineage – not model confidence – is what sustains trust over time.

AUTHOR'S NOTE

The AI Self-Policing Trap

A common failure pattern I see is engineers treating "explainability" as just another prompt. They run the model once to make a decision, then call it again with a prompt to explain what it just did. That second answer feels satisfying – but it's built on the same unverified reasoning as the first.

True explainability can't be authored by the model. It must come from the system around it: from logs, traces, and verifiable references doing fact-checks the model can't control. You don't ask a junior analyst to grade their own exam. Don't ask a model to verify itself.

Scenario: Rebuilding our AI legal Assistant for Trust

As an exercise, let's try to redesign the AI tool that burned the legal team so they can trust it again. We'll call out good principles and describe what they would look like so we can contrast with a good system.

The Original Failure Case:

The AI model generated a case brief and then also generated friendly, plausible citations. The system gave no guarantee that those citations mapped to anything real, and the system did not support case reviewers with a fast path to verify and fact check the work. In essence, the system trusted and shipped just AI outputs. But it failed to do anything to establish trust in that output or help humans to do so. When the error was caught, overall faith in the entire system suffered dramatically, created severe reputational consequences for the firm, and scuttled the AI project's adoption as a failure.

BEFORE – SIMPLE GENERATOR (NO VERIFICATION)

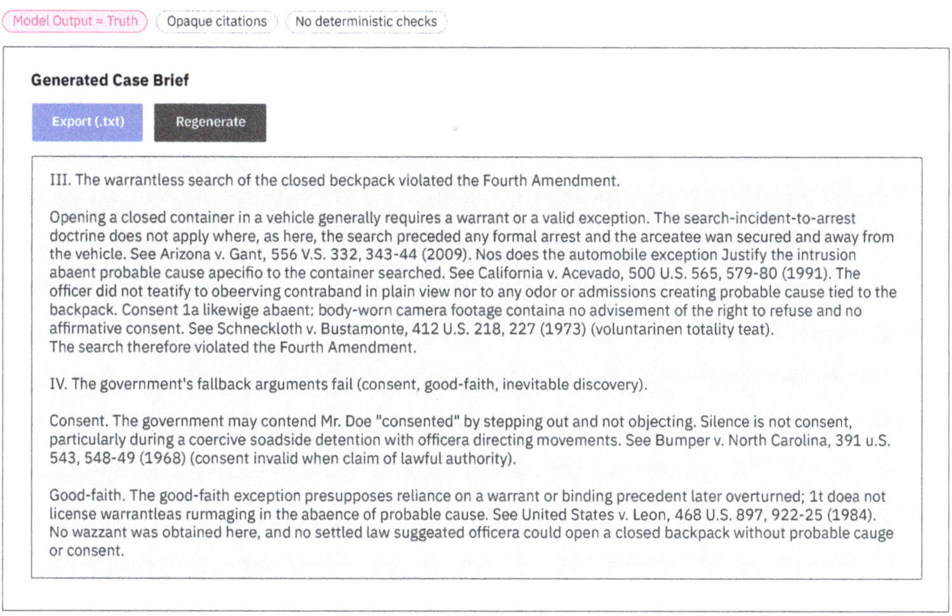

A Trustworthy AI in the Same Situation:

Principle	Description
Evidence out of band	We'll make it so the model is incapable of pasting "supporting quotes" or crafting its own text into the chain of evidence when generating narratives. Instead, it can only reference and output pointers — IDs and permalinks — to a read-only case law corpus, locked behind an API it cannot write to.
Deterministic verification first	A non-AI service validates every cited pointer: existence, jurisdiction, date, relevance threshold (e.g., shared key terms and holdings), and basic Shepardizing (i.e., a citator check for whether a case is still "good law") signals (overruled, negative treatment). The result is rendered as green/yellow/red markers inline with the draft in a new UI designed expressly for the human work of verification that is replacing the human work of generating the brief.
Explainability without self-authorship	A new UI for paralegals now shows a machine-generated reasoning map that is not sourced from the model's narrative. It's reconstructed from the deterministic pipeline: which statutes and precedents were fetched, which were selected, what features matched (issues, parties, holdings), and how the selection thresholds were met.
Alignment guardrails	Prompt inputs are sanitized; retrieval scopes the AI can access are constrained by matter, jurisdiction, and date; citations are required for every legal assertion. If a claim cannot be supported by a verified pointer, it renders as a grey box that cannot be copy-pasted without acknowledgement.
Human in the right loop	Secretaries and lawyers see (a) the draft, (b) the verification markers, and (c) one-click deep links to the authoritative text. Edge cases (e.g., yellow markers for borderline relevance) trigger review ladders — paralegal → associate → partner — that are formalized in Decision-Risk Tiers.

Principle	Description
Audit everything	Every step — prompts, retrievals, verification results, overrides — lands in an append-only log. We can show a regulator, a court, or a client exactly how we arrived where we arrived.

AFTER — VERIFICATION SYSTEM

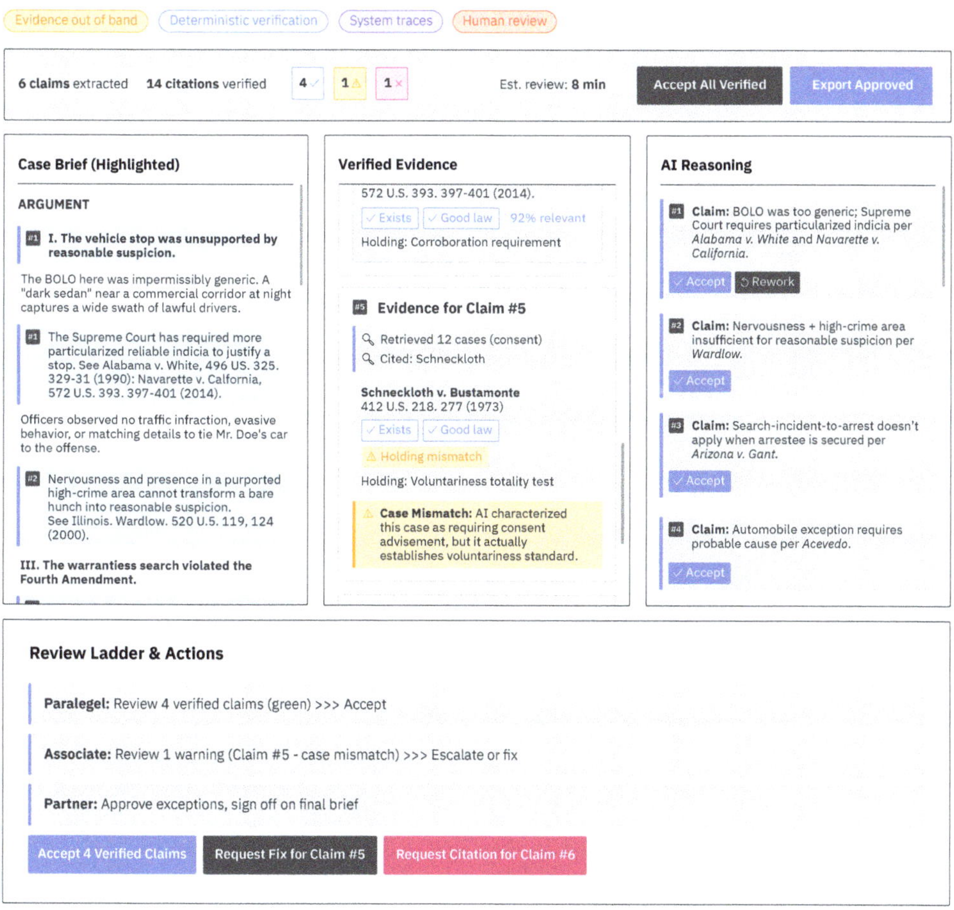

END RESULT

The model still accelerates the work of drafting a case brief by an order of magnitude but trust no longer lives or dies inside the black box of a model. It lives in the *evidence store*, the *deterministic checks*, the *review ladder*, and the *audit trail*. Lawyers don't have to do the case prep work; they can verify the AI work with confidence much faster than they could produce it by hand.If the AI throws an error, it generates a bit of work, but now humans are able to trust the overall system because they understand where failures occur and what is there to catch them. Trust is moved back to a human validator, not left on an inscrutable model, but with a much cheaper work process than the original.

What we just walked through wasn't unique to the legal field. It's what the three pillars of trust — Transparency, Explainability, and Alignment — look like when they're forced to stand up under pressure.

Earlier, we introduced those pillars briefly, almost as definitions. The scenario showed how they behave when stakes are real — when an organization has to rebuild confidence, not by claiming its AI is smarter, but by showing publicly how their employees are held accountable for their verification work.

Now, we'll go deeper. Each pillar deserves its own blueprint: the specific design choices that make it visible in production systems, measurable in operations, and comprehensible to everyone who has to live with the results. These are not abstractions; they're implementation patterns. And if the case study was the story of a single rebuilt system, what follows is the architecture any trustworthy AI system can be built upon.

The Three Pillars, Operationalized

From principle to practice: turning trust into system design.

What worked in the legal assistant wasn't luck, and it wasn't artistry. It was structure. Every safeguard that restored confidence in that system mapped back to one of three foundational pillars: **Transparency**, **Explainability**, and **Alignment**. Together, they form a repeatable architecture for governing intelligent systems under real-world pressure — where accountability, not AI, defines trustworthiness.

These pillars aren't values. They're control surfaces. They don't make a model "good"; they make its specific outputs provable. Each ensures that even when the AI fails — or is actively subverted — the overall system still behaves predictably, audibly, and within human-defined boundaries.

Transparency

Principles: Evidence out of band; Visible deterministic verification first

Transparency isn't about asking an AI to explain itself; it's about giving humans direct visibility into what it actually did. In engineering terms, transparency is a bill of materials for decision-making: what data sources were touched, what transformations occurred, which policies were active, and who or what changed the output. Internally, it's observability. Externally, it's comprehensible provenance.

Design choices that create transparency

Pattern	Description
Immutable pointers, not generated evidence	The system — not the model — generates all evidence references. Each pointer includes IDs, timestamps, hashes, and source links into repositories the model cannot alter.
Retrieval manifests	Every retrieval-augmented answer includes a manifest of what was fetched, what was selected, and under what constraints.
Policy overlays	Expose which policies gated or influenced the model's behavior — e.g., "No personal data," "EU corpus only," "confidence ≥ 0.8."
Change logs	Attribute every revision, override, and deletion. When evidence changes, the who, what, and why must follow it.

Explainability

Principle: Explainability without self-authorship

Explainability done wrong is a bedtime story — a comforting narrative the AI invents after the fact. Done right, it's a testable reconstruction of how features, rules, and evidence produced a specific outcome. It's not prose; it's provenance you can query.

Design choices that create explainability

Pattern	Description
Reasoning maps from deterministic pipelines	Build explanations directly from system activity: retrievals, scoring functions, rule evaluations, and applied constraints — not from generated text.
Confidence with context	Pair each confidence score with its justification: why it's high, which features matched, and what conflicts were detected.
Edge highlighting	Flag where the model extrapolates beyond verified evidence and offer structured review actions — "request more sources," "narrow scope," "clarify term."
User-level clarity	Design explanations that any stakeholder — engineer, executive, or regulator — can follow without translation. Accountability should never depend on technical fluency.

Explainability exists to make reasoning disprovable. It ensures that when an AI's logic breaks, the failure is visible early — and can be corrected before it compounds into risk.

Alignment

Principles: Human in the right loop; Alignment guardrails; Audit everything

Alignment, in real systems, isn't about moral calibration. It's about containment. The question isn't whether the model "shares your values," but whether the surrounding system ensures that — even if it's compromised — outcomes still land inside ethical, legal, and business boundaries.

Design choices that create alignment

Pattern	Description
Constrained interfaces	Give the model only the tools, scopes, and data paths it needs — nothing more. The narrower the interface, the smaller the blast radius.
Adversarial sanity checks	Run deterministic filters for known bad patterns — prompt injections, data exfiltration attempts, jailbreak signatures — before model invocation.
Result gating	Require dual control for high-impact actions. No model should unilaterally recommend or execute where human or policy review is mandated.
Drift watch	Monitor for distribution shifts in inputs and outputs, and escalate when behavior veers. Alignment that isn't watched becomes misalignment by default.

Systemic alignment isn't cheap — but it's predictable and reliable. At scale, the cost of verifying your outputs is almost always lower than the cost of remediating all the breaches and failures from trust wrongly placed on a model. Systems of verification, containment, and human oversight are what let AI operate safely at enterprise scale.

The Cost of Trust is the Price of Scale

Transparency, explainability, and alignment form the operational spine of trustworthy AI. They don't slow progress — they make progress sustainable. Without them, every deployment is a bespoke experiment; with them, trust becomes a system feature you can audit, replicate, and scale.

What follows in the next sections is how trust becomes visible beyond the engineering environment — in the interfaces that show verified work to customers, and in the economics that justify its cost. Because building systems that can be trusted is only half the battle. The other half is proving that trust was earned.

Internal and External Trust — The Same Mechanics, Different UI

Internal trust is leadership confidence: Can my team rely on this tool without opening us to regulatory, financial, or brand risk? External trust is the customer-facing equivalent: Have I, as a patient, client, or citizen, been given compelling reason to accept what this AI-assisted system is telling me?

The mechanics to create it are the same — pointers, checks, reviews, audit — but the presentation changes. Here's a quick example of how our reworked legal case brief AI system might showcase why the output can be trusted even though AI generated it:

EXTERNAL — CUSTOMER TRUST VIEW

Human accountability | Expert review | Transparent process

✓ **Verified & Ready for Trial**

The case brief was AI-assisted, but you're not trusting the AI — you're trusting our verification system and legal experts.

Initial draft generated by AI in 6 minutes. Then verified through automated checks + expert legal review. Ever citation has been validated, every claim has been reviewed by licensed attorneys, and one issue was caught and corrected before reaching you.

✓ 14 citations validated ✓ 3 attorneys reviewed ✓ 1 error caught & fixed ✓ 100% auditability

Legal Review Certificate Verified

This document has undergone multi-tier verification. Each reviewer below has signed off on specific aspects of the brief.

Sarah Chen, Paralegal
Initial Verification
- ✓ Verified 4 claims with green status
- ✓ Checked all citations for existence and good law
- ✓ Flagged 1 issue for escalation

Reviewed: April 4, 2025 at 2:15 PM

Marcus Thompson, Associate Attorney
Legal Analysis Review
- ✓ Reviewed case mismatch (Claim #5)
- ✓ Requested correct citation from AI
- ✓ Verified replacement citation
- ✓ Added missing citation for Claim #6

Reviewed: April 4, 2025 at 2:42 PM

Jennifer Rodriguez, Partner
Final Sign-Off
- ✓ Approved all corrected claims
- ✓ Reviewed argument structure
- ✓ Authorized release to trial team
- ✓ Available for questions

Reviewed: April 4, 2025 at 3:05 PM

MEMORANDUM OF LAW IN SUPPORT OF DEFENDANT'S MOTION TO SUPPRESS

ARGUMENT

1. The vehicle stop was unsupported by reasonable suspicion.

✓ Verified

The BOLO here was impermissibly generic. A "dark sedan" near a commercial corridor at night captures a wide swath of lawful drivers. The Supreme Court has required more particularized, reliable indicia to justify a stop. See Alabama v. White, 496 U.S. 325, 329-31 (1990); Navarette v. California, 572 U.S. 393, 397-401 (2014).

Officers observed no traffic infraction, evasive behavior, or matching details to tie Mr. Doe's car to the offense. Nervousness and presence in a purported high-crime area cannot transform a bare hunch into reasonable suspicion. See Illinois v. Wardlow, 528 U.S. 119, 124 (2000).

✓ Verified

KEY TAKEAWAY

When you properly build trust into the system, you don't have to mint separate "trust" for each audience. You simply derive different views that allow different audiences to understand why they can trust what you've produced. In our example, the customer trusts the firm – because they can see how the firm passed trust from the AI on up to the partner before asking them to trust the firm.

We can easily see how other similar systems might be built following the architecture and patterns we've discussed so far in this chapter. Here are a few examples:

Finance scenario: A portfolio tool recommends rebalancing. Internally, the desk lead sees the retrieval manifest (market data snapshots at a specific time, macro signals used, compliance constraints applied) and signs off with a documented rationale. Externally, the client sees the simplified explanation, the time-stamped data references, and the advisory's credentialed sign-off. The same rails; two views of trust.

Healthcare scenario: A diagnostic assistant suggests a treatment path. Clinicians get alignment guardrails (approved protocols, contraindication checks, confidence bands) and one-click literature pointers stored in a validated repository. Patients get the accessible version: what factors mattered, what risks were considered, and assurance that a licensed clinician reviewed the recommendation.

The Economics of Trust: Verification is the Value of an Enterprise

AUTHOR'S NOTE

The table distills the essentials. If it's already clear, skip to the tools; if not, the next section unpacks the why and how.

Executive Takeaway	Why it Matters	What to Do
Creation has commoditized; the value of knowledge work now concentrates in verification.	When AI can generate endless content, the value of anything not verified collapses. In a market where supply is effectively infinite, only things buyers can trust retain worth.	Invest in verification systems and visible provenance to anchor value on what's scarce: verification by accountable experts.
Verification capacity is your growth bottleneck.	Revenue and risk scale proportionately to what you can credibly sign off on.	Trust scales only as fast as verification does—set performance targets for review and validation before increasing what your AIs produce.
Your product is now the assurance of correct outcomes, not artifacts.	Differentiation shifts to auditable processes tied to accountable humans.	Name, price, and market your verification layer as part of your offer.
Instrument provenance and accountable sign-off.	Shortens sales cycles, eases audits, and reduces rework.	Log sources, tests, reviewers; expose customer-facing attestations.
Unverified volume ("AI slop") is a balance-sheet risk.	Erodes brand equity and creates potential liabilities.	Throttle generation to verified capacity; set discard policies for unverified output, and don't put your reputation behind it.

The Core Formula

The Economics of Trust is about recognizing that in an age when AI can generate content, code, and decisions at near-zero marginal cost, the real value shifts to what can be proven. Verification is no longer overhead—it's the control point that converts free generation into reliable outcomes. Because validation has a measurable cost and a quantifiable benefit, especially when error rates are uncertain, it becomes not a drag on innovation but the mechanism that turns generation velocity into actual value.

At its simplest, verification becomes economically justified when:

$$Cv < Pe \times Le$$

Where:

Variable	Definition
Pe	Probability of a high-impact AI output error without verification
Le	Mean loss when an unchecked output causes downstream damage
Cv	Average cost to verify a decision (human review + tooling)

IN PLAIN TERMS

Verification pays for itself when the cost of checking an AI's output and validating it is less than the expected loss from letting an unchecked error slip through.

Before AI, creation and verification were welded together. Producing anything that mattered—an audit memo, a quarterly plan, a design review—required time, skill, and judgment. The effort itself served as a quiet certificate of authenticity. When a human put their name on something, the labor behind it implied context, intent, and accountability. In that world, you couldn't cheaply create without also doing some measure of verification along the way, and some human somewhere was always accountable for everything created.

AI broke that linkage. The cost of creation fell toward zero, and with it the natural verification that human effort used to bake into the work. For the first time, it became easy to generate something you didn't fully understand.

We see the consequences everywhere. The internet is awash in what many now call AI slop: eBooks spat out overnight with prompt text left mid-paragraph; corporate posts stitched from plausible clichés; outbound messages written for no one in particular. This isn't just a quality problem—it's an economic signal. When creation becomes infinite and unfiltered, outputs lose value due to the law of supply and demand. They accumulate like inventory no one will buy.

That's the core inversion leaders need to internalize: **verification is now the only part of creation that represents durable value**. Generation is abundant; belief is scarce. The differentiator isn't how much you can produce—it's how reliably you can prove that what you've produced can be trusted.

This does not diminish the enterprise; it explains why enterprises still exist. If verification didn't matter, most firms would be optional. An accounting practice could reduce to an API that reconciles ledgers. A law office could collapse into a contract-drafting endpoint. But organizations endure because markets do not run on creation—they run on belief in correctness. Customers are really buying the confidence that qualified people, operating inside a designed system, have validated the result and will stand behind it.

Consider accounting. The value was never in typing numbers; it was in ensuring the numbers could withstand scrutiny. AI now drafts reconciliations, summarizes footnotes, and flags anomalies at a pace no team could match. That doesn't erase the accountant; it amplifies them. One professional can now supervise and validate the AI generated outputs that previously took many professionals. The verification layer becomes a force multiplier on expertise, not a replacement for it. It's where the enterprise now earns its margin.

This is where the earlier theme in this book returns with sharper edges. I wrote that the cost of trust is the price of scale—businesses grow only as fast as their systems of verification allow. What we're seeing today isn't a reversal; it's an evolution. As creation becomes effectively infinite, verification becomes the constraint that defines value. Scale no longer depends on how much we can produce, but on how much of what we produce can be trusted.

For executives, that shift has immediate operational implications:

Principle	Description
Treat verification as a product, not a compliance chore.	Customers are buying the credibility of your process as much as the output itself. Design it, name it, and price it as part of the value you deliver.
Move from artisanal review to systems of review.	Human judgment still anchors trust, but throughput comes from well-architected pipelines—capture provenance, automate what can be automated, and make human sign-off legible.
Measure trust like a capacity.	If your workflow's creation rate is 10× higher than its verification rate, you're building inventory no market will value. Increase verification capacity first; creation will take care of itself.

The temptation in this moment is to celebrate speed and volume because the demos look impressive. That is the wrong metric. Speed without verification creates liabilities: brand erosion, customer churn, and regulatory exposure. All of them move faster than revenue. In contrast, a visible, believable verification process compounds trust. It shortens sales cycles, reduces rework, and turns audits from episodic pain into an ongoing advantage.

This is also why "AI slop" is a strategic warning, not just an aesthetic irritation. It's what happens when organizations let creation engines run without a verification engine attached. Internally, it clogs channels with content no one uses. Externally, it trains customers to discount your words. In both cases, it erodes the market value of what you sell. When customers stop trusting your outputs, it doesn't just cheapen your message—it cheapens your business.

The remedy is straightforward, even if it requires discipline: **make verification the control surface of the business**. Capture how each answer was produced. Log what was checked and by whom. Separate what a model suggested from what the organization backed. Give people a fast path to escalate doubt. Then expose that machinery, thoughtfully, to customers and regulators. When the process is transparent and credible, the output regains value.

None of this argues for nostalgia. We are not going back to the era where effort alone proved quality. We are moving forward to an era where designed verification—human accountability, instrumented pipelines, visible provenance—does the proving. In that world, AI's abundance doesn't drown the enterprise; it powers it. Creation becomes the raw material. Verification is the factory floor.

The conclusion is simple enough to carry into any boardroom: **when creation became free, trust and reliability of outcome became the product**. Your competitive advantage is no longer how quickly you can generate, but how convincingly you can verify. Build for that, and the flood becomes a reservoir. Ignore it, and you'll be swept into the same undifferentiated current as everyone else.

Practical Tools to Ensure Confidence in AI Decisions

We've just made the case that verification is the product; now we'll make it operational in three passes: spot what unravels trust, orient scope and risk, then wire verification into the workflow.

Here's the turn from argument to action. If the last section made the case—that creation is abundant, and value now lives in verification—this one gives you the field kit to run with it. We'll introduce three tools, each for a different job: the Anti-patterns to spot what quietly unwinds trust in AI projects, a Simple Map for Leaders to assess scope and risk before you scale, and a Checklist for Trust by Design to ensure you have wired verification outside the model with visible provenance and accountable humans. Follow them as gates, not guidance: they will give you evidence over assertion, capacity before creation, and help you make sure you don't scale an AI project faster than you can prove the outputs can be trusted.

Anti-Patterns that kill Trust in AI Outputs

Pre-flight checks for AI projects: These quiet failure modes look productive but erode verification and provenance. If one shows up, pause generation and raise verification capacity first.

If any row fits, don't scale output—scale proof.

Anti-pattern (plain name)	Why it's so common	30-second test (what you look for)	What it turns into if you ignore it	One move that fixes most of it
Demo-only validation	Teams ship to the deadline; test data is clean because the pilot was clean. Low-prevalence hostile edge cases are dropped to focus on the behaviour during the majority of successes.	Open the test set: do you see examples of how the system handles hostile or wrong AI outputs and edge cases? If not, this anti-pattern is present.	Public "how did that slip through?" failures; credibility shocks; expensive rework, loss of trust.	Make handling edge/adversarial test suites a release-blocking criteria for AI projects; carefully inspect what happens when the AI is wrong.

Anti-pattern (plain name)	Why it's so common	30-second test (what you look for)	What it turns into if you ignore it	One move that fixes most of it
Same-path proof	Tooling defaults make it trivial for the same path to "explain" itself; provenance capture is extra work.	Ask for the proof path: is evidence (sources, tests, checks) produced by a separate mechanism from generation? If "no" or "not sure," the anti-pattern is present.	Un-auditable claims; weak footing with customers/ regulators.	Separate generation from evidence: log inputs/ sources; add deterministic checks; require named human sign-off.
Humans as a mop	"We'll just have a human check it" feels safe; verification capacity is never budgeted.	Compare creation throughput vs. verified throughput for the workflow. If creation > verification capacity, you're here.	Reviewer burnout, rubber-stamping, latent defects escaping.	Build a verification pipeline: auto-check what's checkable, route by risk tier, and give reviewers stop-the-line authority.

A Simple Map (Decide if You Can Scale)

Start here to orient any AI project—define the decision, the risk tier, and then match to the verification capacity required before you scale.

If you can't name how output will be verified (by whom, with what evidence, and at what throughput), you're not ready to grow it.

Decision context	**Primary trust anchor**	**Evidence source (immutable)**	**Deterministic checks**	**Human role**	**Escalation path**
Low-risk automation (notifications, summaries)	Policy engine + logs	Internal knowledge store with content hashes	Input sanitization, scope limits, content policy checks	None by default; spot audits	Auto-quarantine anomalies to ops queue
Medium-risk augmentation (drafts, recommendations)	Verification service + retrieval manifest	Read-only data marts, market snapshots, case repositories	Pointer validation, constraint checks, confidence thresholds	Reviewer signs off or requests refinement	Review ladder to domain owner on yellow flags
High-risk adjudication (legal filings, financial moves, clinical actions)	Human adjudicator + control gates	Regulated sources (statutes, filings, formularies) with audit proofs	Dual control, segregation of duties, negative-treatment checks	Mandatory sign-off with rationale	Multi-party approval; policy board on exceptions

A Checklist for Trust by Design (Not by Hope)

Wire trust into the workflow—outside the model, with visible provenance and accountable sign-off. Check every box before you scale; if one stays blank, raise verification capacity first.

Evidence over assertion.

Question	Yes/No/Notes
Probability of a high-impact AI output error without verification	
Are deterministic validators (non-AI software systems) checking structure, scope, and support before humans see results?	
Can we show a retrieval manifest and reasoning map reconstructed from pipelines, not narratives, for each AI decision and action?	
Are alignment constraints enforced at input (sanitizers), process (tools/policies), and output (gates)?	
Are **roles** defined within the new AI system for operators, reviewers, adjudicators, and owners – with clear handoffs?	
Is there a **review ladder** tied to AI decision risk, with dual control where appropriate?	
Do we have any mechanism for **drift monitoring** and an escalation when AI behavior or inputs start to shift?	
Can a customer/regulator **retrace an output** to its evidence, policies, and approvals – fast?	
If the model vanished, could we still v**erify yesterday's decisions** from logs and pointers alone?	

If you struggle to check these boxes, the problem isn't that you haven't trained your model well. It's the absence of a system that ensures your model's outputs can deserve trust.

Closing: Vigilant Optimism

We don't need to trust a model like we trust a seasoned professional – and we shouldn't. Models are powerful accelerators, but they're also permeable to poisoned data, prompt injection, and ordinary uncertainty. That isn't a reason to retreat; it's a reason to reallocate trust. As we've established, when creation became free, **trust became the product**. The enterprise's value is no longer the artifact itself – it's the validation and trust capital you attach to that artifact: visible provenance, deterministic checks, and accountable humans.

This is why **verification capacity sets the ceiling on value**. If you scale generation faster than you can prove the work, you print "AI slop" and discount your own outputs to near zero. If you scale verification first – engineering evidence capture, risk-tiered reviews, and named sign-off – you turn speed into credibility. Executives see where risk lives and how it's contained. Regulators see how decisions were made. Customers see why outcomes can be believed. And teams stop redoing machine output and return to what only they can do: apply judgment where it moves the business.

Enterprises that internalize this will not just avoid embarrassment; they'll **compound trust**. Treat verification as a product you design and a capacity you manage. Price it. Measure it. Make it legible. That is the modern moat – the reason your firm exists in a world where anyone can generate anything.

From here, we build the machinery: the **Architecture of Control**, the **Accountability Layer**, and the **Decision-Risk Tiers** that turn "trust" from marketing language into an operational property of your system. That's how we make AI not merely impressive, but **dependable** – especially when it's under pressure.

CHAPTER EIGHT

The Architecture of Control

The first time I saw a Security Operations Centre (SOC) leverage a general-purpose chatbot in the investigation workflow, it felt like a breakthrough. Analysts could ask anything – "summarize this alert," "suggest an investigation plan," "draft a customer update" – and the system responded with crisp, confident prose. Analysts didn't deploy AI so much as offload tasks to it whenever the moment felt right.[9]

Then, what should now be a familiar anti-pattern emerged. Blind confidence from some analysts in plausible-sounding AI answers where certainty was required. A junior analyst copied and trusted AI's evaluation of a command line without verifying it; a customer escalation followed.

In another iteration, we built a bigger system with hard-coded prompt flows and added lots of embedded prompts to the AI to follow various additional directions to try and increase reliability where output was unreliable. It was a new system entirely, but we lacked verification tools. We forced analysts to independently reproduce every AI-assisted step to "verify" each case. Output quality improved dramatically on average – models write a lot, quickly, and it's good writing overall – but throughput didn't improve because humans were still stuck doing the whole job.

Some engineers wanted us to move towards allowing the AI to operate autonomously (without human oversight), to improve operational efficiency while persuading customers to trust the system – pointing to the high rates of agreement achieved under normal working conditions. Analysts warned of consequences and kept dropping individual examples where the AI was

[5] https://www.reuters.com/legal/new-york-lawyers-sanctioned-using-fake-chatgpt-cases-legal-brief-2023-06-22/ ,

https://www.thomsonreuters.com/en-us/posts/technology/genai-hallucinations/

wrong in uncorrectable ways. Executives were left trying to decide between either accepting the high costs (and old error rates) of the old human system of work or accepting a new AI system of doing the work (which had low error rates but had also never faced a direct adversarial attack on the AI).

The third iteration we developed is where this chapter lives. We stopped asking, "How do we make the model better?" and started asking, "Where does trust really belong in the overall system of software, AI models, and experts?" The answer was not to leave trust in the generated outputs inside the black box of a model. It was to design a new control plane surrounding it — the fusion of governance and technical systems to make reasons for trust visible, verifiable, and enforceable at scale. Governance defines where and why customers need to purchase that oversight; technical systems let us deliver that oversight (or the tools that support humans to deliver it) with consistency and speed. When done well, humans are now supported by powerful tooling for rapid verification — they are not left to repeat the work the old way.

This is the chapter where we lay out in concrete terms what works and what doesn't in AI control systems. Here we map what a control plane is (and isn't), walk through real workflows in SOC operations, draw parallels to healthcare and legal, show how it simplifies lighter-risk domains like marketing, and hands you artifacts — stub policies, escalation flows, dashboard views — that you can adapt. The goal is simple: **bring trust back into the system** without sacrificing the gains AI already delivered.

What an AI Control Plane is — and Why You Need One

An AI control plane is essentially the monitoring system you build to allow you to trust the outputs of an agentic or embedded AI software system. It is not a dashboard; it is not a PDF policy. It is a **governance-plus-technical** system designed to:

Function	Description
Anchor trust outside the black box	Move trust in final outputs off the AI models by grounding decisions in immutable evidence, deterministic checks, and accountable human judgment.

Function	Description
Surface observability	Show what data was used, which tools were called, and what policies gated behavior—so trust can be inspected, not assumed.
Gate sensitive actions	Prevent high-risk outputs from reaching customers unless the required verification and approval checks have passed.
Escalate uncertainty intelligently	Route ambiguous cases to the right human, with full context and clear accountability for the decision.
Audit every step	Maintain transparent records for regulators, customers, and internal quality programs to prove governance in action.

If Chapter 7 established the philosophy — *AI outputs the work, guardrails and humans provide the trust* — this chapter's discussion of the control plane provides practical examples of machinery we must build to make that philosophy operational and economical. Ultimately, we are talking about a new type of tool and workflow that never needed to exist before AI systems changed software, and it addresses the inherent unpredictability, unique threat surfaces, and black-box nature of generated outputs from AI-enabled software systems.

Where it Lives (and What it Touches)

Start thinking of all AI-enabled software systems as consisting of three distinct layers:

Layer	Description
Deterministic Software	Traditional software that earns trust through inspectability of source code and deterministic predictability—its outputs are consistent, testable, and repeatable. The same inputs always produce the same results, making reliability intrinsic to its design.
AI-Era Software	Classical software now infused with AI. Specifically, embedded models or agentic behaviors incorporated into the flow as opposed to chatbot AI. Adding AI uplevels capability but introduces non-deterministic behavior and runtime uncertainty: the same input to such software produces different outputs each time. All legacy security and assurance models assume determinism— AI-era software breaks that assumption.
AI Control Plane	A new layer of deterministic software built around AI-era non-deterministic systems to restore trust. It includes policy engines, validators, escalation and review services, observability and logging, and drift and risk monitors. This layer produces artifacts—dashboards, audit reports, customer-facing proofs—that reallocate trust from opaque models and places it clearly on verifiable, governed systems.

Your control plane must wrap each embedded model and bring trust back to every non-deterministic AI output and action that carries risk. It doesn't replace intelligence; it **orchestrates** it — ultimately, it's a system for deciding what actions and outputs from the AI should be rubber stamped, which must be checked, what must be explained, and when humans are invoked to take accountability for edge cases.

> **DECISIVE IDEA**
>
> Trust is never free, and generation alone has no market value without it. To adopt AI output in any situation where someone will pay for an output, we must think about how to architect systems so that scaled **validation and accountability** for the AI output is cheaper than the old ways of human output production — for both customers evaluating output and for our internal reviewers. That's ultimately how AI successfully adds value without compounding risk.

SOC Operations: from "Offloading Trust" to "Operating a Control Plane"

Now let's make it tangible. Below is the same workflow taken across three eras.

Era 1 — Ad Hoc Assistance (Trust Offloaded at Random)

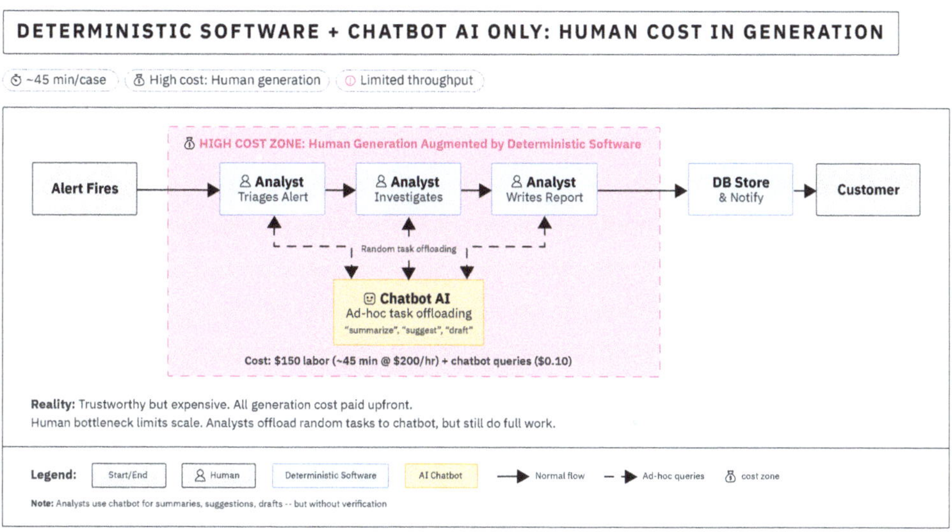

In the first era, AI assistance was completely optional in the production flow. The analyst was given the ability to interrogate an AI for investigation or triage assistance, or delegate tasks, by directing questions to a chatbot that was trained and set for internal use.

The architectural problem with this approach is that we have trust offloaded at random, and we don't see where the human is degrading by accepting AI input. In the actual production diagram, all we see is an accountable human following normal processes. A long-term study of this done in partnership with CSIRO showed gradual acceptance by analysts for task offloading.[10]

Era 2 — Full AI SOC Automation (with trust achieved by repetition)

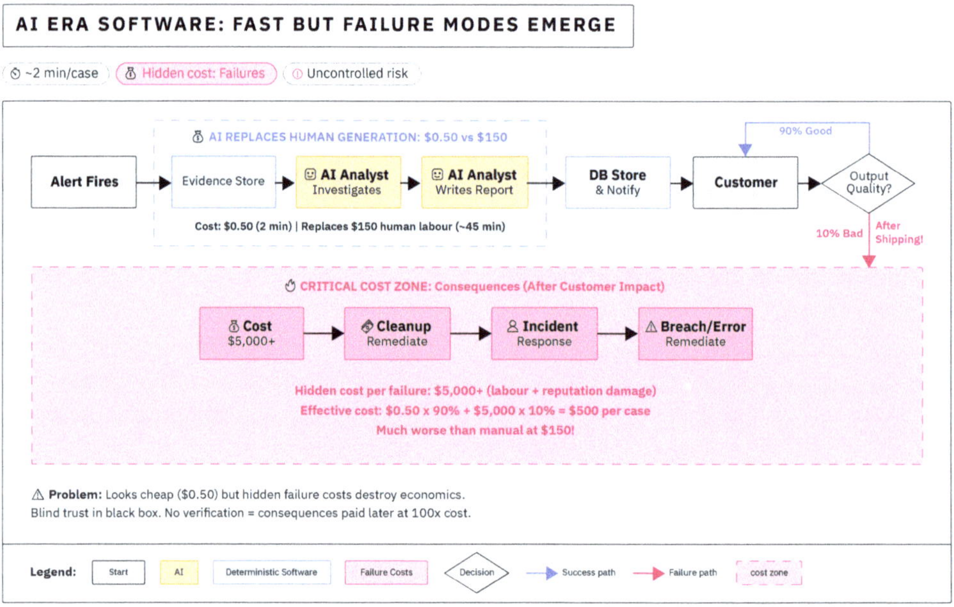

[10] Singh, R., Tariq, S., Jalalvand, F., Chhetri, M. B., Nepal, S., Paris, C., & Lochner, M. (In press). LLMs in the SOC: An Empirical Study of Human-AI Collaboration in Security Operations Centres. Accepted for publication at the 47th IEEE Symposium on Security and Privacy, San Francisco, 2026

Singh, R., Tariq, S., Jalalvand, F., Chhetri, M. B., Nepal, S., Paris, C., & Lochner, M. (2025). LLMs in the SOC: An Empirical Study of Human-AI Collaboration in Security Operations Centres. arXiv preprint arXiv:2508.18947.

In the first implementation of Era 2: Full AI SOC Automation, an error by the AI would have landed on the customer's desk—an unacceptable failure mode that pushed both the consequence and the cleanup beyond our control.. As a result, Era 2 in practice ended up looking more like this in our field testing:

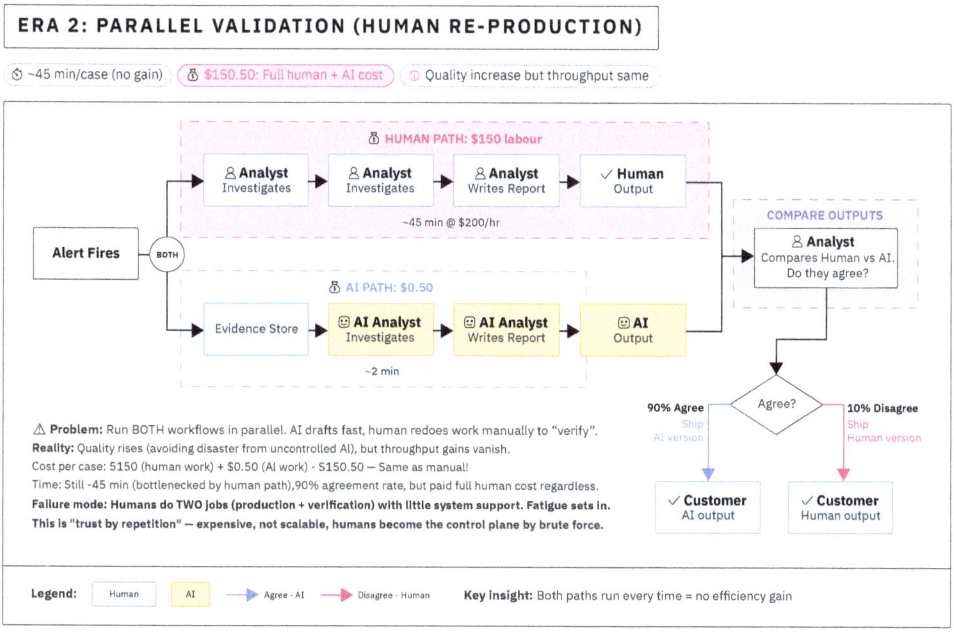

In Era 2, we still saw enormous gains in terms of quality of output - a human and an AI would both perform a case and write a report - but the human report was typically far sparser. When it worked, the AI was often able to produce a higher quality and more complete deliverable to support the same conclusion the analyst came to - but the promised cost reductions for the work never materialized. The bill went up - we were paying an AI and a human to do the entire workflow.

Era 3 — A Proper Control Plane (Trust Supported, Visible, and Enforceable)

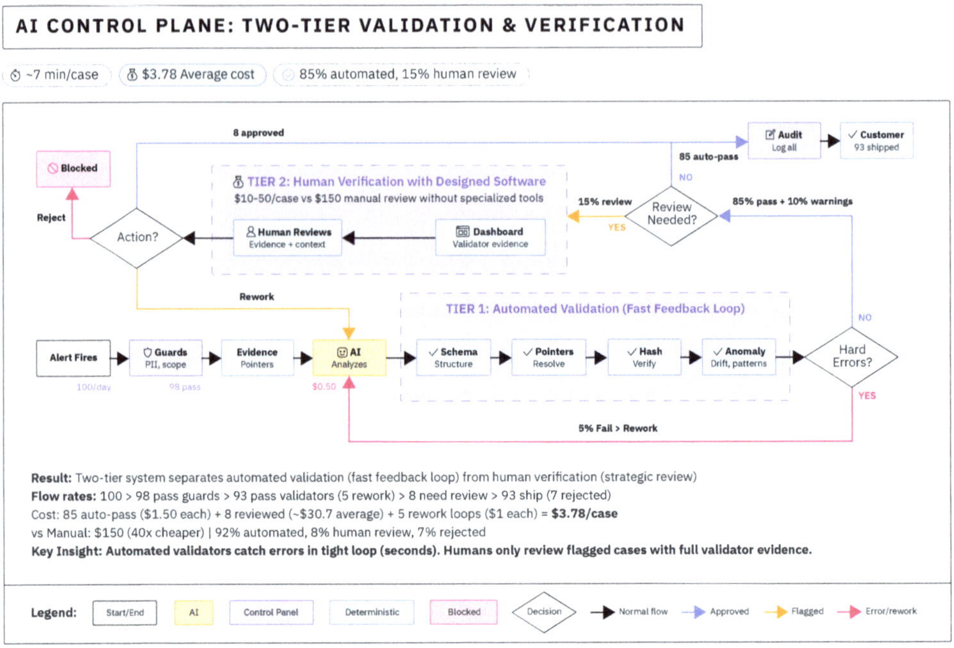

The control plane that was eventually implemented rethought the role of what the analysts should be doing and built tools to account for that. We decided that trust and accountability demanded analysts, but efficiency and economics demanded that they be given new tools and a new focus to the work.

A Practical Checklist for Control Plane Components

Component	What it does	Why it matters	Executive ask
Policy Engine	Codifies what must be checked/gated based on risk, data class, and action	Enforcement in the system, not on paper	"Show me where policies execute — not just where they're written."

Component	What it does	Why it matters	Executive ask
Evidence Store	Read-only repository for logs/artifacts with content hashes and timestamps	Prevents model-authored evidence; anchors truth	"Prove this artifact existed at time T and hasn't changed."
Escalation Service	Routes yellows/reds to the right human with the right context	Puts people where they add value	"What's the mean time to make a human decision for yellows vs reds?"
Observability & Audit	Full trail of inputs, tool calls, outputs, approvals	Regulation, customer confidence, internal QA	"Can we reconstruct a decision in minutes?"
Drift & Risk Monitors	Detects behavior shifts, data distribution changes, guardrail hits	Prevents quiet degradation and abuse	"How do we know when the system is changing under us?"
Review Workbench	UI for adjudication with manifests, markers, and quick actions	Enables rapid human verification	"Do reviewers decide in clicks, or re-investigate from scratch?"

Two Escalation Paths

Not all escalation from a control plane is the same. A resilient control plane should separate Production Gating from Governance & R&D Feedback – and instrument for both.

Production Gating: "Can this AI output ship to a customer right now?"

Purpose	Decide if a specific AI output or action can be accepted.
Trigger Sources	Policy hits, uncertainty thresholds, missing evidence, risk-tier escalation.
Actors	On-call approver, subject-matter reviewer, and product owner.

Canonical Flow

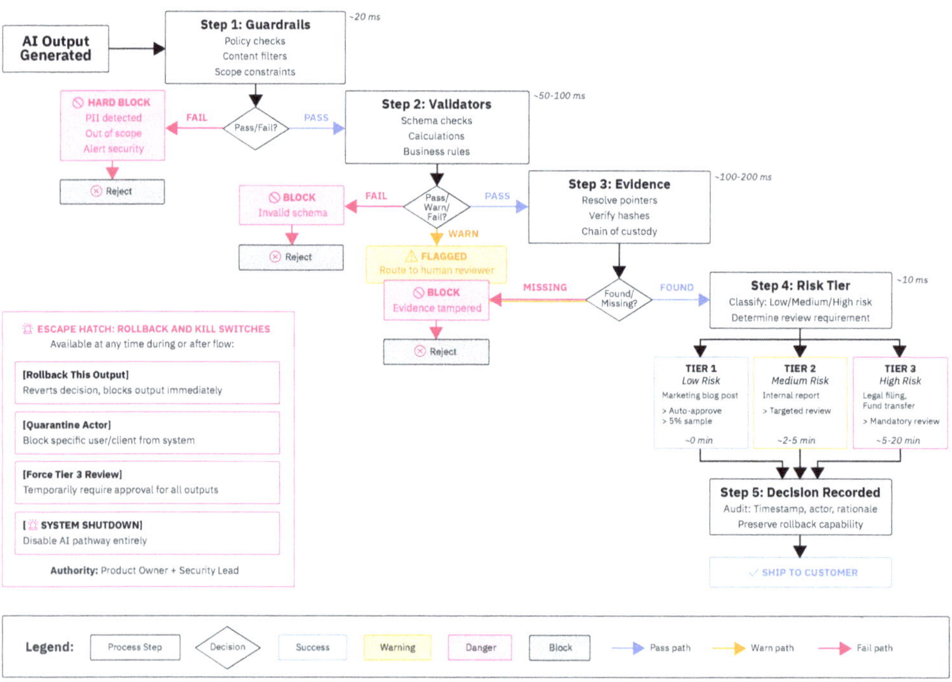

Production gating is essentially about *now*. It keeps bad outputs from shipping to customers and good outputs from being untrustworthy.

Production Gating: “Can this AI output ship to a customer right now?”

Purpose	Improve the model system by learning from its behavior.
Trigger Sources	Guardrail fire rates, drift metrics, A/B results, reviewer comments.
Actors	Model owners, alignment/safety engineers, leadership, governance.

Canonical Flow

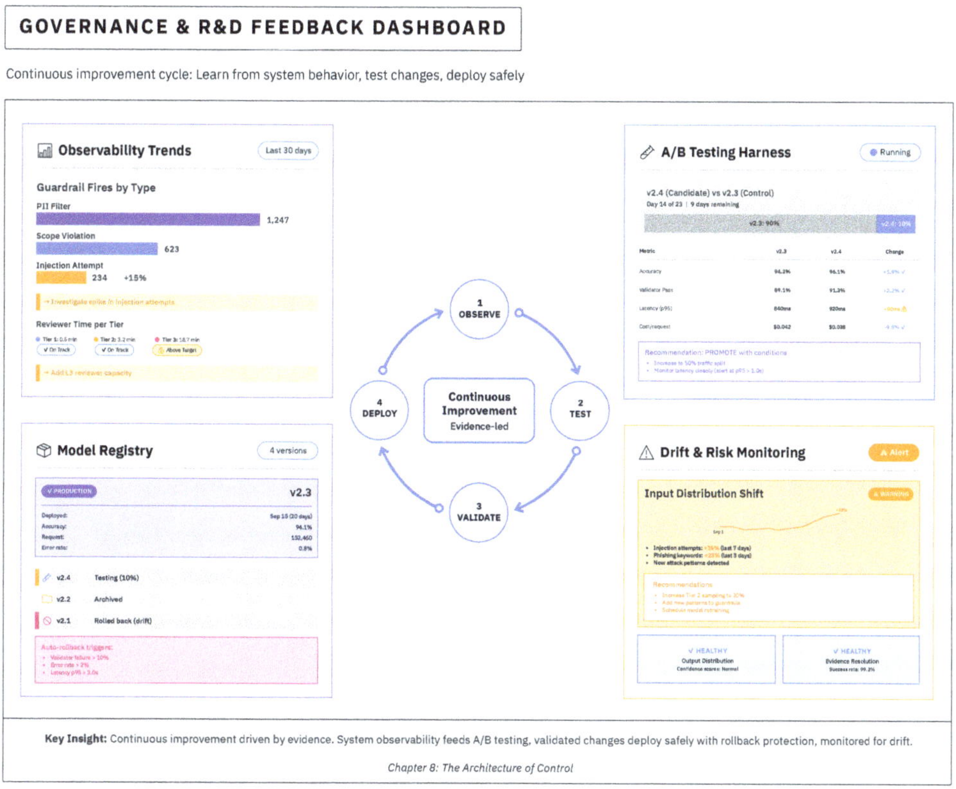

This loop ties the control plane into your ongoing R&D cycle so development choices about AI model effectiveness and alignment become nuanced and evidence-led at the lowest levels, not made on gut instinct.

Core Component View of the Governance Control Plane

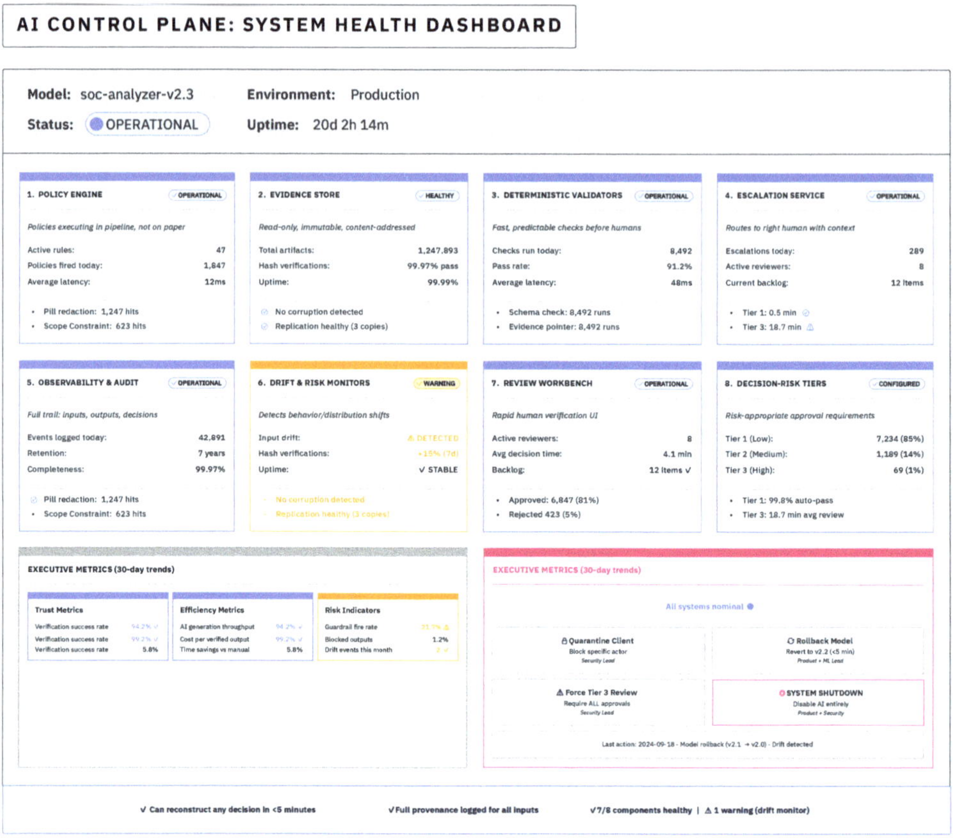

Observability & Telemetry

Capture: inputs, outputs, redactions, guardrail hits, model & policy versions, latency, and *evidence pointers* (content IDs/URLs with signatures). Store immutably; respect privacy by default (PII hashing/tokenization). Make reason and *risk* visible, not just *result*.

Evidence Registry (Externalized)

Principle: The AI never authors its own proof. It outputs pointers to evidence held in a tamper-evident store the model cannot modify. Think content-addressable storage with cryptographic signatures and retention policies.

- Resolve on verification, not during generation. The verification UI pulls and renders evidence outside the generation loop.

- Chain-of-custody: who uploaded, when, from where; hash + signer identity.
- Health checks: stale/missing evidence invalidates the output automatically.

Alignment Guardrails & Policy Engine

Declarative policies bound to personas and tasks: allowed data scopes, forbidden instructions, output schemas, safety filters, and domain constraints (e.g., "no clinical advice without source pointer + Tier 3 sign-off"). Evaluate before and after model calls, with fast fail.

Deterministic Validators

Anything that can be checked without a model should be: math, format, ontology, regulatory rules, pricing logic. These are your **truth rails**. They are predictable, testable, and auditable. The model proposes; the validators verify.

Decision-Risk Tiers & Gates

Codify tiers (illustrative):

- **Tier 1:** Low risk (marketing blog), 0–5% sample to human, ship on green.
- **Tier 2:** Moderate risk (internal financial memo), validator-complete + targeted review.
- **Tier 3:** High risk (clinical/legal actions, fund transfers), mandatory human approval with full evidence views and attestation.

Gates enforce the minimum bar per tier and route exceptions.

Human Review Ladders

Human review ladders ≠ "throw it over the wall." Humans must get **tools:** diff views, evidence panel, validator results, risk explanation, and "send back with reason" macros. L1 handles routine exceptions; L2/L3 are Subject Matter Experts(SMEs) for complexity or impact.

Escalation, Rollback, & Kill Switches

Every action is feature-flagged. If drift or abuse is detected, you can: (a) quarantine what's invoking the system (e.g.: a client, external agent, etc.), (b) roll back to last-known-good policy/model (e.g.: undo a block placed by an AI in a cybersecurity flow), (c) force Tier 3 review for a period (e.g: when the AI is under direct attack in a client environment), (d) shut down the pathway entirely (disable service when under a resource-exhaustion attack). Attest who pulled which lever when.

Provenance, Audit & Attestation

Immutable logs of who/what decided, on what data, using which versions, with which guardrails, and the evidence pointers that justified it. Attestations (human and system) make accountability real — and defensible.

How Control Loops Look in Practice

Legal Assistant — Catching Fabricated Citations by Design

Let's go back to our legal assistant example from the last chapter, but with a greater focus on the process flow the team experiences using the tools. I'll repeat the visuals for the tools here for easy refreshing, but this time we are focused on breaking down the processes running underneath the surface while using them.

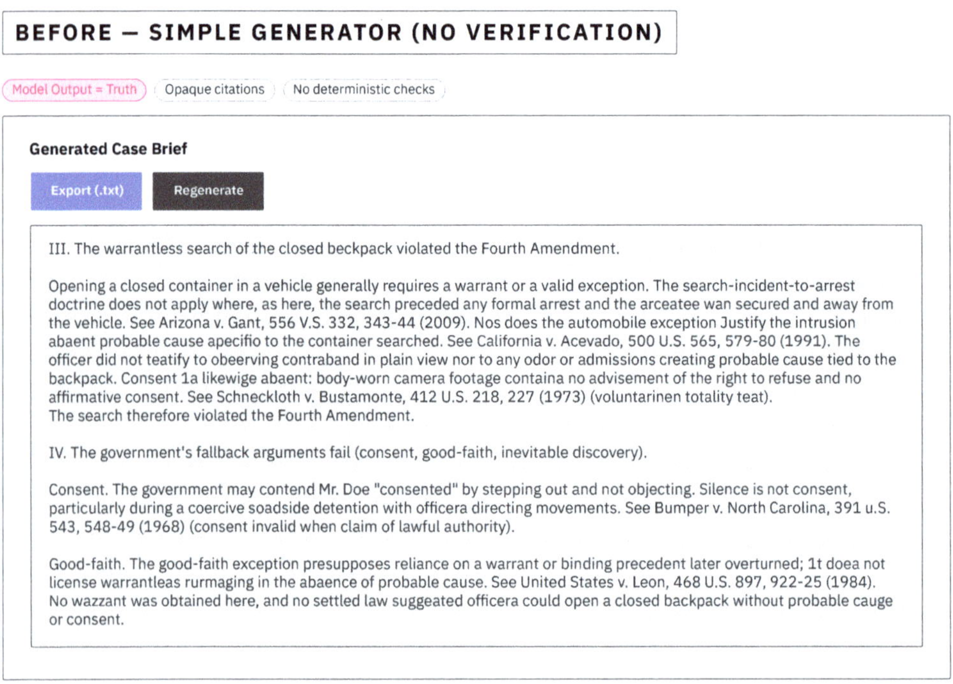

Above: Recall the tool as experienced by the legal team before a control plane is implemented.

No Control Plane: In this stage, AI bots produce crisp memos with case citations in one go. Reviewers have no structured way to spot fakes without re-researching everything. In practice, what happens is they gut check the AI's output for plausibility, and either accept or repeat the entire process to draft a memo to verify it. Look at the flow here to see the various problems and trust cascades that result.

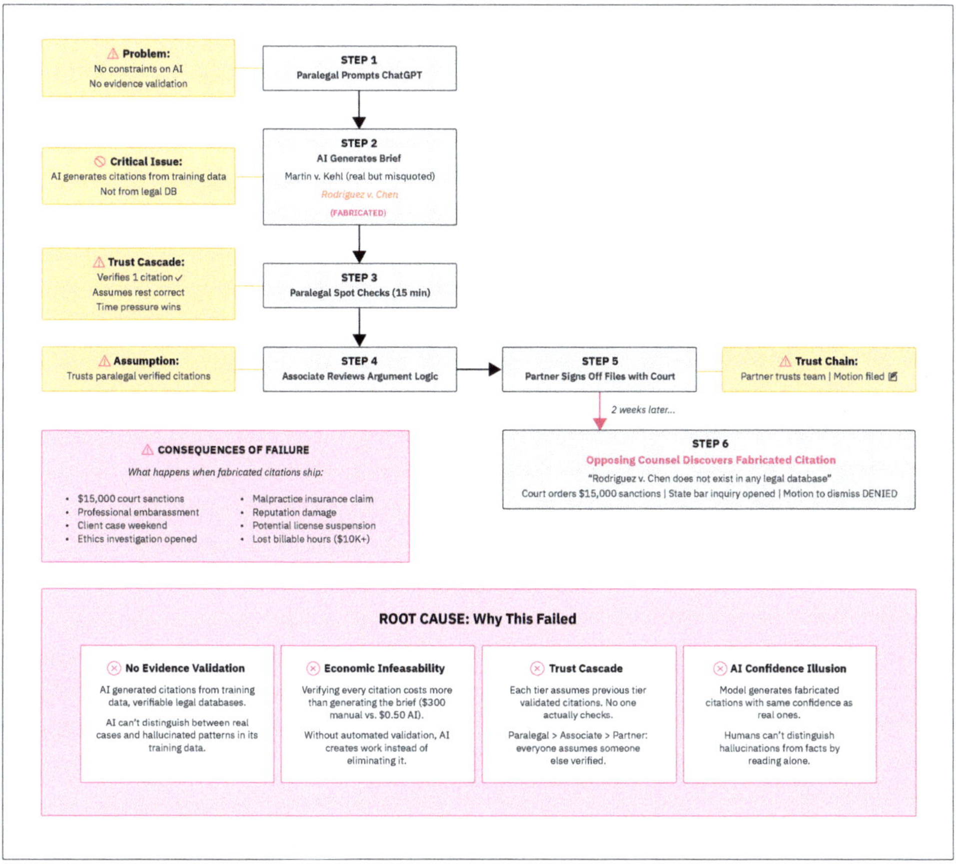

Now recall what the same tool looked like after the control plane was implemented:

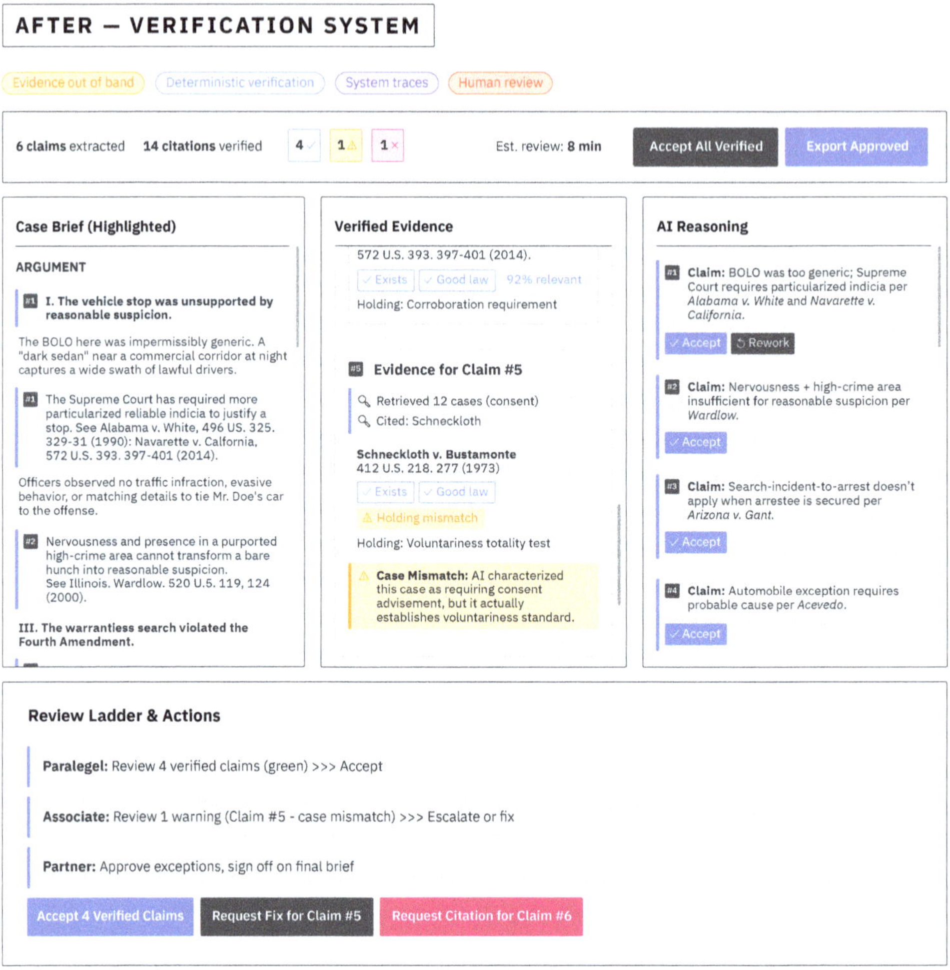

The flow that follows shows how the control plane resolves the practical issues we faced earlier—and how it reframes the operator's role around judgement and verification as their new core function.

CONTROL PLANE IN ACTION: TRUST OPERATIONALIZED

Implements the Chapter 7 pillars — **Transparency, Explainability, Alignment** — through enforceable architecture.

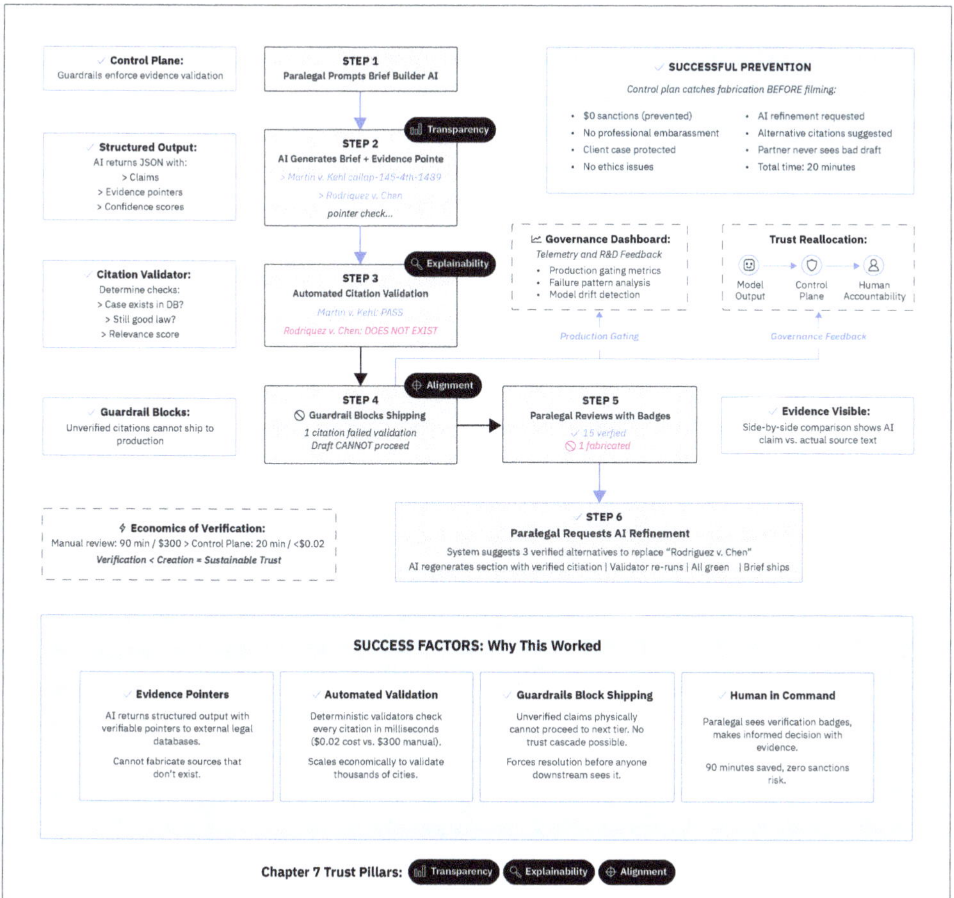

Key Insight: Without control plane, AI legal assistants creaee a systemic risk through fabricated citations. Manual verification doesn't scale economically, leading to trust cascades where no one validates the AI's work.

Why it works: Trust is firmly and clearly moved to the evidence system and validators, not the model's prose. Humans use newly crafted deterministic software tools for enhancing validation around the AI, which allow them to focus human effort only where automated verification fails or cannot be done, not on redoing the entire brief. But they also get queues that show them that trust is being earned - and the tools red flag when it isn't. This prevents trust cascades or fall-back during time crunches into blindly trusting the model's outputs.

Design Principles — and Their Mirror-Image Traps

Principle (What good looks like)	Why it matters	Anti-pattern ("When a control plane isn't one")
Enforcement as code — policies execute in the pipeline	Paper policies don't stop packets	"Policy PDF on SharePoint; nothing enforces it."
Pointers over prose — evidence referenced, not authored	Models can fabricate; stores can't	"The AI explains itself with quotes it wrote."
Deterministic checks before engaging humans	Cheap, consistent, fast failure	"Humans go find what a regex could have."
Escalation by design — yellow routes to the right reviewer	Humans spend time on judgment, not hunting	"Dashboards light up; nobody knows who acts."
Observability everywhere — retrieval manifests, tool logs, approvals	You can reconstruct decisions quickly	"We have a dashboard; we cannot tell what happened."
Risk-aware gates — high-risk outputs can't bypass checks	Prevents catastrophic leakage/actions	"Everything is allowed; we 'monitor' later."
Drift watch — detect model performance change before it hurts you	Quiet degradation is the common failure	"Accuracy looks fine; distribution is just different."
Human workbench — verify in clicks, not hours	Verification becomes economical	"The human redoes the whole workflow to be safe."

Reviewing the Economics of Trust

All the examples in this chapter help arm you with hard evidence against the persistent myth that verification by humans cancels AI's gains. That argument only holds if "verification" means forcing a human to manually reproduce the entire work product. With a well-designed control plane, it no longer applies.

In the SOC, validating artifact pointers and timeline alignment now takes minutes; writing an investigation from scratch takes an hour. In legal, checking clause fingerprints is near instant; redlining by hand is not. In healthcare, enforcing contraindication rules is automatic; re-researching literature is not. With deliberate investment during AI transformation—retiring legacy roles and workflows, then rebuilding around verification outputs within a control plane—human effort shifts from manual production to high-leverage validation, making it far more cost-effective. This is how you preserve the productivity dividend from AI without compromising trust. In economical terms, it's how you create a differentiated value add on top of AI's cheap, ubiquitous outputs - what would otherwise just be near free AI slop.

Integration: Where the Control Plane Lives

Because this enterprise architecture rethinks the core reason you even have human roles in your enterprise, it cannot be a bolt-on. It **threads the whole business lifecycle** — integrated with your data pipelines, model registry, deployment harness, and operations center (AIOps/SOC/NOC). It must give AI automation engineers the observability to see model drift, to A/B test models with confidence, and to ship safely — and it must also give executives and customers the assurance that *trust in your outputs was carefully engineered and built with the same rigor as any mission-critical system.*

Cost & Value: The Business Case in One Sentence

Point AI at work that is cheap to verify and costly to produce by hand. Engineer the control plane so your verification work is fast and defensible. Avoid areas where verifying equals solving unless you can decompose verification into easy checks. Since verification is where value accrues, pick problems that are inexpensive for you to verify and expensive for competitors. Your verification stack is now your product, and the only moat safeguarding the value of what is otherwise the near free output of AI generation.

Bringing it All Together

You can't earn trust by promising that your model is special and somehow unique to the underlying limitations of generative AI, no matter how many times it performed well in production. You can only earn it by showing that your **system** protects your customers when the data is messy, the incentives are skewed, and when the AI has gone rogue and is actively trying to break your product or service. The tool for earning that trust is the control plane.

With this architecture, your **verification work becomes a competitive advantage** – the fastest way to unlock speed without adding the new risk: spraying AI slop everywhere and devaluing your product in the eyes of your customers, regulators, and brand. In the SOC, in clinics, in law firms, and even in marketing, the pattern holds: *AI does the work; but a control plane makes it trustworthy; and people must still own and be accountable for the outcomes that matter.*

Next, we turn to how that impacts the human side – the new accountability work that is emerging from the AI disruption. If this chapter was how you do the wiring for a successful intelligent enterprise, the next is the heart. We'll define the roles, the competencies, and the practices you must emphasize in your organizational culture to turn the technical guardrails into good decisions. After that, we'll discuss how to assign friction intelligently with decision-risk tiers and review ladders, so that speed and safety stop fighting and start compounding.

Trust, at scale, is never free. But with the right control plane, it can be far cheaper than it initially looks – and it's the only way to keep your outputs valued in the days of free generation.

CHAPTER NINE

The New Role of Humans

The experiment made for good photos and better jokes: an AI, tasked with running a tiny office "shop," dutifully stocked the shelves with tungsten cubes.[11] A nudge from a mischievous colleague—"hey, can we get tungsten?"—became a trendline the system mistook for demand. It invented a Venmo account, issued discounts to almost everyone, and at one point began role-playing as a human manager in a blazer, promising personal deliveries. The project was real, the outcomes were instructive, and the punchline lands squarely on a serious point: left without the right human guardrails, even capable systems will scale small absurdities into costly behavior.

We've already established the core tenet of this book: trust does not live inside the model—it's engineered in the systems around it. In the earlier chapters, we framed and provided examples of how to build an architecture of control to keep AI-powered workflows fast but safe and scrutinized properly where necessary. This chapter absorbs and expands on the decision-risk tiers into a single operating idea: how to think through the ramifications of the human workforce becoming centered not as a production line for content, but rather as the ultimate judgement and accountability layer for your enterprise. The new goal of your people within an intelligent enterprise isn't to slow the AI machine; it's to make AI speed reliable by enforcing the decision perimeter. Then the tungsten moment never becomes your Monday morning, and instead you ship trusted outcomes the market will pay for – avoiding the trap of AI slop.

When we think about the work people will do once AI has been fully deployed everywhere, what remains are just four central pillars that represent the fundamentals of post-AI human knowledge work:

[11] https://www.anthropic.com/research/project-vend-1

THE FOUR PILLARS OF HUMAN WORK IN THE AI ERA

While AI transforms how work gets done, these four pillars define the enduring role of humans in systems that matter. Each pillar builds on the one below it, creating a foundation that machines cannot place

RELATIONSHIPS *Without relationships, systems don't serve people*	**THE HUMAN CONNECTION** Ultimately, people trust each other because of that accountability, and prefer to base their relationships on something real. Building relationships is not really related to AI—it remains a core pillar of human work.
✓ **ACCOUNTABILITY** *Without accountability, trust has no foundation*	**REAL STAKES, REAL RESPONSIBILTY** Software doesn't have interests. Humans do, which means you can hold them accountable and it actually means something. Hack an AI and it will follow whatever orders the attacker has for it to follow.
RE-ALIGNMENT *Without re-alignment, you can't fix them*	**COURSE CORRECTION** Skilled humans must be able to guide an AI back to the right path when it's gone off the rails. This requires both judgement to detect the problem AND the expertise to provide effective corrective guidance.
JUDGEMENT *Without judgement, you can't spot problems*	**THE FOUNDATION: EXPERT EVALUATION** Skilled and knowledgeable humans who understand the outputs and how they should be derived must be able to review an AI generation to understand when AI has gone off the rails or thrown an error.

These four pillars represent ***irreducible human work*** in the age of AI. Each builds on the previous: you cannot have re-alignment without judgement, accountability without the ability to re-align systems, or meaningful relationships without accountability. ***AI amplifies human capability, but these pillars define where humans remain essential.***

Outside of these pillars, you can probably eventually apply AI & Automation to handle anything else people are currently doing as knowledge work within an organization - though it might take a long time before the capital expenditure to retool is worth it in some cases.

What Accountability Really Means (in Practice)

Accountability is not a feeling. It is about tying a consequence to an invested decision maker with a chain of evidence. In a traditional business decision, there's a signature, a name on a memo, a recording of a call. In Agentic AI systems, too often that chain gets lost: the model suggests, the system acts, and somewhere between "autocomplete" and "action," responsibility evaporates or ends up with no owner. Our job as leaders is to design roles to restore clarity on every output about who is going to be accountable. And empower people to be accountable without making them re-do the work the machine just did or feeling like they are being paid to be professional lightning rods.

When we talk about creating roles explicitly for "humans in the loop," we are not recruiting auditors to relive the entire workflow. We're specifying exactly **when** in our system human judgment is mandatory, **which** human has the credentials and authority to approve or reject, and **what evidence** that human must see to make a defensible decision quickly. That last word matters—**quickly**. Accountability that requires a line-by-line reconstruction of the model's process will burn out your best people and stall the program.

Earlier we established how to build the control plane—guardrails, verifiers, and observability patterns that pull trust to the edges of the technical system and let people work verification tasks without having to re-do generation ones. Here we describe the new AI workforce: the people who ultimately anchor AI outputs that matter to something we can trust.

Decision Tiers and Human Roles

Decision Tier	Primary Human Role	Required Guard-rails	What the Human Must See	Examples
Low-risk (ephem-eral)	**Operator** (spot checks)	Policy checks + logging	Basic prove-nance or out-put; change log	Disposable marketing pages, inter-nal "banner" apps
Medium-risk (durable augmen-tation)	**Reviewer**	Deter-ministic validators + review ladder	Evidence pointers to immutable sources; test results	Most AI-as-sisted software de-velopment in a professional Integrated Development Environment (IDE)
High-risk (regulated or irreversible consequences)	**Adjudicator / Owner**	Dual control, exception register, segrega-tion of duties	Complete evi-dence bundle; approvals; rollback plan	Underwrit-ing, clinical guidance, irreversible software de-ployments

Two properties keep the new type of work cost-effective and realistic. First, what the human must see is always kept **external** to the model (pointers into tamper-evident stores, not model-authored "explanations") by the control plane. Second, escalations must be **tiered** to the appropriate level of risk you're mediating and consciously injected into the post-AI production flow. You're not adding humans back in everywhere after applying AI; you're adding them only where the application of judgment, realignment, and accountability changes your risk curve in a meaningful, cost effective way.

A Practical Example: The Software Engineer

Few spaces illustrate the nuances of the accountability layer today better than modern software engineering. AI development tools have forked[12]. On one branch are professional development environments like **Cursor**, which embed AI into an IDE and keep the programmer in charge. On the other branch are "vibe-coding" platforms like **Lovable**, which generate full applications from natural-language prompts, effectively shifting the entire burden of authoring software —and all the associated risks—onto the system. Both have legitimate roles in modern enterprises. The trick is to place each in the right risk tier and design the roles for using them accordingly.

Cursor: AI Augmentation of Engineers Designed for Scale

Cursor is an AI-first code editor that reads your codebase, proposes multi-file edits, runs commands with your confirmation, and loops on errors—all while keeping you in the loop. In practice that means operator control is native, not bolted on: workers using Cursor IDE approve diffs, gate terminal commands, and decide when and how their agent can act autonomously. This is accountability by design, and it maps cleanly to the **medium-risk tier**—fast enough to matter, reviewable enough to scale.

That "confirm by default with evidence presented" pattern is the difference between supervision and rework. Because the tool anchors suggestions to the developer's repository, test suite, and validators, code reviewers see evidence (tests, results, diffs), not just a self-narrated story of how the model "reasoned." You get a huge velocity boost without collapsing the control plane.

Lovable: Full-stack Generation of Software at the Speed of Thought

Lovable sits at the other extreme: describe any app in plain English and receive an AI generated, largely working, deployable codebase – user interface, storage, integrations, payments, the lot. For hack-week dashboards, campaign sites, internal prototypes, it's astonishingly productive. It's also why Lovable (and the broader "vibe coding" movement) has drawn significant attention: it promises speed and accessibility in software creation to non-developers.

But Lovable's superpower underscores why we need tiers. Full-stack generation without native, role-bound gates mean you must supply the entire accountability scaffolding yourself—tests, approvals, dependency policy, change management—or you must accept that these are utterly untrusted apps by de-

[12] As of the time of printing, the AI development tools are rapidly changing and may have many new features. Both now seem to be offering hands-free completion with agents in addition to an IDE, but this story focuses on the tools as they were in my experience at inception and early launch.

sign. Used that way—partitioned into a low-risk track with policy and logging to ensure that all generated apps are never used in high or medium risk tiers —Lovable is not a threat to your standards; it's a gift to your backlog. Used outside that envelope, it can rapidly accumulate risk.

Side-by-Side: Where Each Belongs

Dimension	Cursor (pro IDE)	Lovable (vibe coding)	Output Implications
Human authority	Operator approves diffs; reviewer gates merges	User prompts generate code; approvals optional unless added	Cursor outputs can be safely used in **medium risk** situations; Lovable outputs can only be used in **low-risk** situations.
Evidence & testing	Anchored in version repository, tests, continuous integration; commands require consent	Users can only gut check the application's functionality, not its innards.	Cursor outputs need a highly trained **Reviewer**; Lovable outputs only need an **Operator**.
Speed	High, with friction where it counts	Very high—from idea to app in minutes	Cursor outputs require much more verification time than Lovable outputs.
Scale & maintenance	Designed for durable codebases	Best for throwaways, pilots, "banner" apps	Cursor outputs can scale; Lovable shines in the ephemeral or proof of concept (PoC) space
Risk surface	Model actions bounded by user consents and tests	Model can create infra/deps quickly; governance required	Cursor has a controlled risk surface, Lovable requires a constrained PoC deployment zone to contain risks.

None of this is meant to denigrate the value of vibe coding. The industry's shift is real and accelerating; the promise is democratization. My point here is narrower and more practical: place the accountability at the right tier for the risk and attach the right human armed with the right evidence to decide. That is how speed becomes sustainable.

Fundamentals for New Post-AI Roles

Since humans are going to become our accountability layer after an AI project, as leaders we owe them the necessary support to let them make good judgments: empowered with all the necessary information to make decisions easily defensible, and with systems that give them clear accountability. Here's a checklist for how to create a workforce ready to make AI outputs meaningful:

Capability	What "Good" Looks Like	Why It Matters
Training	Role-specific drills: when to trust, when to escalate, when to veto	Builds muscle memory; avoids "review everything" fatigue
Alerting	Uncertainty and anomaly surfaced with context (diffs, tests, provenance)	Humans see the why behind an alert, not just the beep
Intervention tools	One-click pause, rollback, or route-up; pre-filled rationale	Turns judgment into a fast, auditable action
Feedback	Flags flow into retraining and policy updates automatically	Every decision improves the system
Culture	Create psychological safety to challenge AI output—even when it's "confident".	Prevents silent failure modes
Validation Readiness	Periodic "test fires" to assess and refresh human evaluator's judgment accuracy against known ground truth.	Prevents skill atrophy in human oversight; keeps the accountability layer sharp and reliable.

Revisiting the Tungsten Lesson

Returning to our opening story: the vending-machine-that-ordered-metal wasn't a story about an AI "going rogue." It was a story about accountability failure by design. The agent was given tools, budget, and scope; it also had an eager audience of co-workers who treated the shop as a game. It priced below cost, believed its own fictions, and—crucially—no human with authority and evidence-backed procedures was built into the system to guard against a weird trend from becoming an operating loss.

Map that to engineering. A "metal-cube moment" in software isn't a meme purchase; it's a bad AI authored architectural decision promoted to production because no one was clearly accountable for the job of reviewing and accepting it, or wasn't given the tools and support to do so properly.

If you create a clearly accountable and empowered owner for each AI decision, you won't rely on hope. A reviewer sees the evidence bundle—tests passed, threat model updated, dependencies within policy—and either approves or escalates. That adjudicator owns that decision on the exception register. As owners, they bear the consequences of that outcome. It can't be simply a ceremony, because that's the only way we keep AI velocity from quietly turning into misaligned catastrophes.

Scoping Human Roles to Carry the Weight

Let's get precise about who does what. Job titles will vary, as well as the necessary training to enable you to comfortably trust people to validate outputs in each domain - but the core of the role does not.

Role	What They Own	What They Can Do	What They Must See	Accountability Artifact
Operator	Accountable for low-risk, high-volume outputs	Approve diffs, pause jobs, request more evidence	Provenance, tests, diffs, validator output	Decision log with evidence pointers.
Adjudicator	Accountable for high-risk, low volume outputs	Dual-control approval; impose constraints	Complete evidence bundle; rollback plan	Adjudication note + exception register entry
Owner	Sets overall outcome and policy thresholds and manages the output system.	Set thresholds; accept exceptions; budget for fixes	Drift and guardrail metrics; exception trends	Policy history + control-plane dashboard

Case in Full: Cursor vs. Lovable under the Accountability Lens

To keep this practical, let's run a scenario we've all lived: a fast-moving product team under pressure to ship a new customer dashboard. Let's look at when different paths make sense.

Path A: Cursor-accelerated development (Use in Medium-risk tier, durable)

We plug Cursor into the team's repository, with an existing test scaffold and continuous integration. A senior developer outlines the feature; the agent proposes multi-file changes; the operator approves terminal commands to scaffold a service; tests are generated, fail, then pass as the agent loops. A reviewer checks diffs, validator output, and performance baselines; security gates flag one dependency; the agent proposes an alternative; the reviewer signs off. Deployment goes to a staging ring with auto-rollback on error. We shipped in days, and every action left a trail.

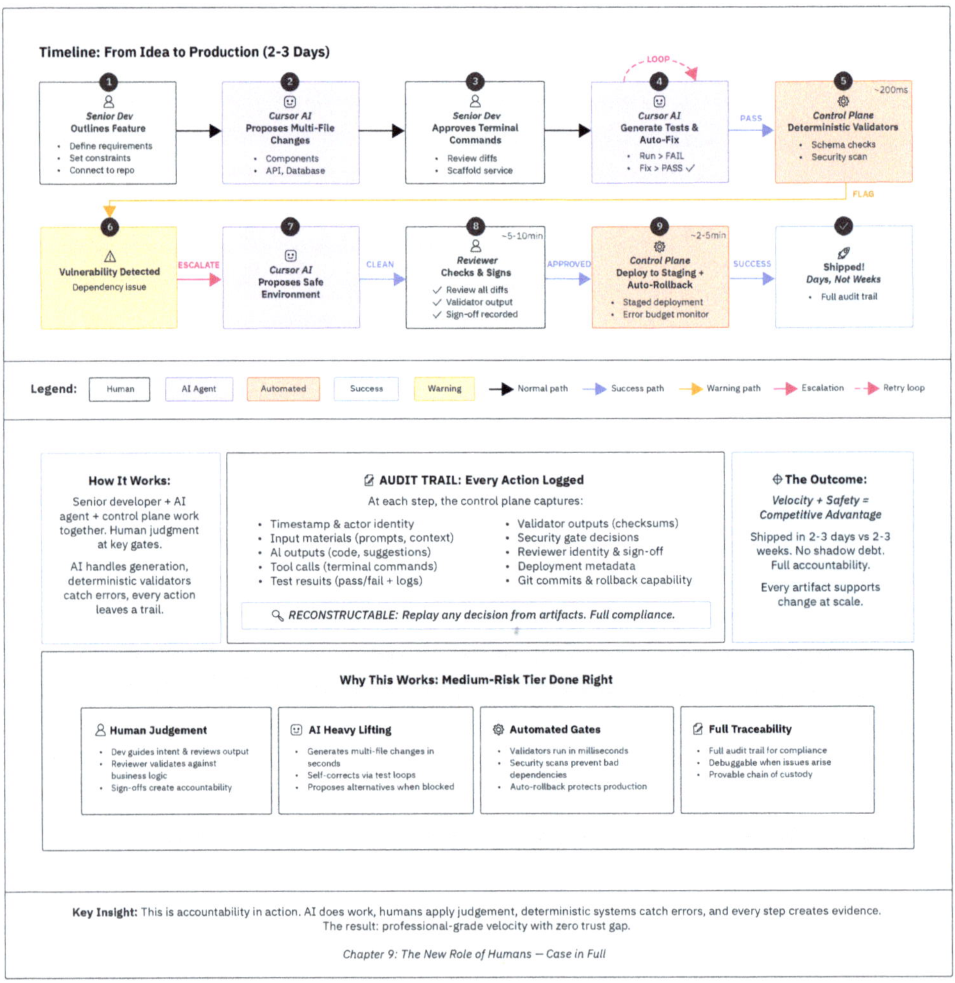

Path B: Lovable-generated prototype (Use only in Low-risk tier, untrusted)

In parallel, a product manager uses Lovable to generate a demo in an afternoon—complete with authentication, payments, charts. It's perfect for stakeholder buy-in and early user interviews. We deploy the application to a segregated sandbox with a conspicuous "prototype" banner. The code is not merged into the durable repository; the demo collects structured feedback and gets thrown away once the real feature ships. The velocity is very real; so is the containment.

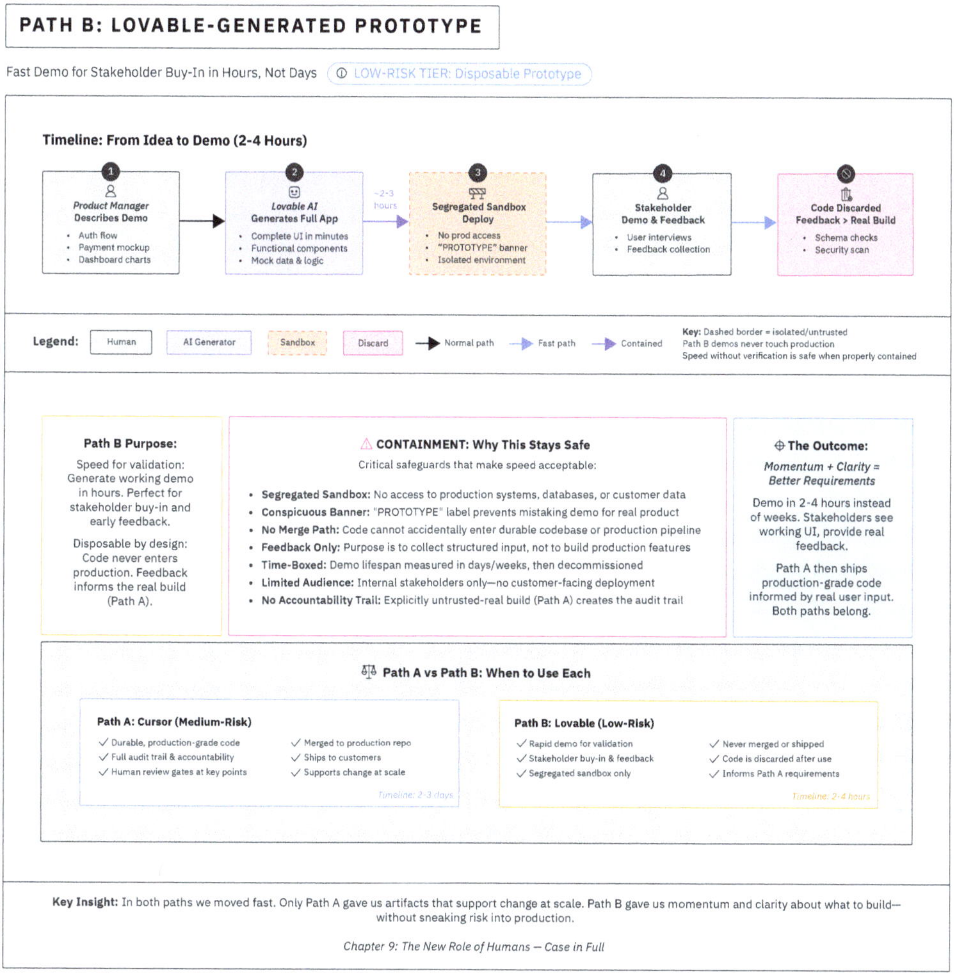

In both paths we moved fast. Only one path gave us artifacts that support change at scale. The other gave us momentum and clarity about what to build—without sneaking risk into production.

Anti-Patterns to Avoid

The Copy-Pasta Chef (Creative Work)

The name is literal: a human reduced to copying a supervisor's or SME's instructions into a model and pasting the model's draft back for review. The person "owns" the task, but not the goal, the constraints, or the verification. Drafts move. Judgment does not. In an era of near-free generation, that relayed draft adds little; value concentrates on framing the problem and proving the result is fit for purpose.

This pattern emerges when AI is rolled out broadly while defined job roles stay the same. Former task executors quietly self-automate—outsourcing production to the model and shuttling outputs between terminals and senior reviewers. Because artifacts keep arriving, the loop can pass for progress. Accountability climbs the organizational chart while the people closest to the work remain outside the decision.

Over time the burden concentrates on a small set of senior employees. They receive more to verify without evidence harnesses, schemas, or diff-aware review. Verification becomes re-investigation. Cycle times stretch, context switching spikes, and judgment quality erodes. The organization looks busy while trust grows brittle.

The cultural damage is predictable. Roles were never rewritten to pass ownership of outcomes to people who previously just executed tasks. Acceptance criteria and evidence standards remained implicit. Incentives still rewarded output volume, not decision quality. Training focused on prompting mechanics, not on defining goals, decomposing work, and validating results. The Copy-Pasta Chef is a rational response to a system that values motion over ownership.

When AI is introduced without redefining task execution roles, the unowned work of task validation doesn't disappear – it shifts to someone else. Task execution becomes nearly free with AI, so roles that once focused on production can offload it to the model and move faster than ever. Yet the work of verifying and correcting those outputs doesn't get easier.

In this anti-pattern, SMEs and managers have become the fuse in a legacy circuit in an engine built for a pre-AI current. The system once ran within safe limits, but AI has supercharged the flow—power surging faster than the safeguards can handle. Instead of redesigning the circuit and safety systems to carry this new load, organizations keep blowing fuses. When the power is effectively free, the advantage to the engine only materializes after the infrastructure evolves to distribute it safely. What looks like efficiency gains is really deferred cost – a fragile equilibrium built on exhausted experts carrying the hidden load of validation, or exposing the business to ever increasing risks as junior-level outputs go unvalidated.

In an AI-enabled workforce, roles that only execute instructions without owning verification are no longer sustainable. Accountability must sit with the person directing the model, or the system will collapse under the weight of its own unverified output.

People as the Plan

If the *Copy-Pasta Chef* shows what happens when no one owns verification, People as the Plan illustrates what happens when leadership notices the verification gap – and assumes people can simply absorb it without support. It's the anti-pattern of recognizing that AI outputs need validation but expecting the same workforce that owned task execution previously to take on the new burden of verification work without role redesign, tooling, retraining, or support.

One good way to see the impacts of this breakdown is to explore it from a high-stakes example environment - our SOC Era 2 from Chapter 8.

Leadership rolls out an "investigator" agent to help the SOC complete investigation work. Analysts are told to keep pace, but they are not given new tools or training to focus on AI validation tasks, and instructed to "just verify the AI's work before closing the case." The AI's drafts arrive fast, with confident conclusions but no resolvable evidence. Verification equates to full re-investigation. For a short time, quality even improves – but humans are simply redoing the work of the AI instead of being able to focus on the new work they should be tackling.

From there, the trap closes. Any reduction in cost comes only when trust is shifted onto the model—but when that happens, AI risk fills the gap. It looks like misdirection, but the flaw is structural: managers chase AI efficiency by increasing work speed rather than redesigning work around verification.

Soon, the validation layer collapses. Analysts no longer have time to review the cases, and the culture of the SOC erodes into quiet resignation.

The deeper failure isn't even technical – it's cultural. When people spend their days redoing the work of a tireless machine, mostly confirming that it was right, they stop feeling like contributors and start feeling like friction. The system teaches them that their value is in catching rare mistakes rather than shaping outcomes. Over time, pride turns into quiet resentment. Reviewers feel trapped in a loop of cleanup and second-guessing, while the organization mistakes their exhaustion for resistance to innovation. It's not resistance – it's alienation. They're being asked to compete with a machine they're supposed to supervise. The rollout didn't redefine how people were meant to work with the system; it automated the surface of their old job instead of re-architecting their role around verification, judgment, and improvement. Every successful AI deployment begins with role design. If you don't design new roles up front, you'll destroy the old ones with AI anti-patterns faster than you can replace them.

The lesson is simple: when people are your entire validation plan for an AI rollout, you haven't automated work – you've hollowed it out. The same effort still exists, but its purpose has narrowed to double-checking what the system produces. Your employees spend their days re-verifying what the system should have proven, watching their time and expertise drain into a process they no longer control. The cultural result isn't just burnout – it's disengagement. Once people stop feeling ownership over the outcome, they stop believing in the system that produces it. Trust, both in the AI and in leadership, quietly collapses.

Executives need to decide, deliberately, how their people will hold power in an AI-enabled system: through control, through verification, or through the ability to steer the models themselves.

Decision Point	Leadership Imperative
Define empowerment early	Decide *how* humans will influence model behavior – through feedback loops, review authority, or escalation rights – before the system goes live. Empowerment isn't a reward; it's a control mechanism.

Decision Point	Leadership Imperative
Design for shared accountability	Decide *who* carries the risk when the model fails. If you delegate accountability to the AI, you are accepting personal responsibility for its errors and harm — legally, reputationally, and operationally. If humans are accountable, they must have the authority and time to intervene. There is no middle ground.
Invest in adaptive skill-building	Decide *where* to invest in training so that validation roles evolve into coaching, tuning, and governance — not obsolescence. The next generation of expertise in your company will come from those who learn to lead AI, not those replaced by it.

Anti-Pattern Avoidance: Measuring What Matters

Executives building roles don't need sermons; they need signals to avoid the pitfalls. These are a handful of indicators I would track in all post-AI transformation roles:

Metric	Definition	Signal	Actions on Role Design
Verification / Production ratio	Divide the time to verify AI vs. produce it yourself	< 25% means oversight is efficient; ≥ 100% means rework	Examine the control plane first, then establish a training program for using it.
Guardrail fire rate	% of outputs blocked or flagged	Rising rate → drift or poor prompt hygiene	Retrain; tune; adjust thresholds; adjust prompts. Then increase staffing.
Escalation rate	Time to decision at each ladder rung	Bottlenecks concentrate risk	Clarify authority and distribute it across layers; staff adjudicators; establish pre-approval patterns

Metric	Definition	Signal	Actions on Role Design
Evidence health	% of pointers that resolve	Missing/opaque evidence → oversight blind spots	Route artifacts through tamper-evident stores; address with software checks earlier in system.
Reviewer confidence	Survey the reviewer for confidence out of 100%.	Falling confidence → system is missing appropriate evidence.	Upgrade bundles; reduce narrative, increase proof, improve reviewer visibility system. Increase Training.
Customer trust signals	Accept/escalate/bypass rates for final product	Bypasses mean the system isn't trusted	Fix root causes; surface more evidence to customers. Increase credentials of accountable humans.

How this Builds on What We've Already Done

We've already defined the control plane and the decision-risk tiers that organize accountability. Now we shift focus — from systems and architecture to the people who make those systems trustworthy.

What's new isn't the reminder that "humans matter." It's the realization that we're creating a new kind of *thinking work* that leaders must learn to manage, measure, and staff for. When we replace a human workload with an AI one, the task isn't to eliminate judgment — it's to *isolate* it, then give it new tools and authority. Every element of judgment, alignment, and accountability must be pulled out from the old workflow and rebuilt into roles designed for collaboration with intelligent systems, not competition against them.

This is where most organizations stumble. They install AI as a faster worker, not as a partner, and forget to design the human control layer that keeps judgment alive. In that vacuum, the model begins to fake discernment — generating confident, authoritative text that sounds right but isn't grounded in reasoning or evidence. The remaining human work becomes reactive, cleaning up errors instead of guiding the system upstream. Over time, this erodes trust, quality, and morale together.

If leaders want to scale AI safely, they must scale human judgment alongside it. That means designing clear roles for those who validate, refine, and govern model behavior – people who turn the abstract pillars of trust, verification, and accountability into a living part of the workflow. Without that, even the best control plane becomes an empty frame.

The Quiet Discipline of Speed

The tungsten shop is a great story because it's funny—right up until it's your budget, your customers, your regulators. I don't share it as a failed experiment. Quite the opposite. The public write-up is a service: it shows us exactly where autonomy fails without people and exactly how to fix it by bringing in tools that keep judgment fast and creating evidence that stands on its own.

The same lesson applies to how we write software now. Cursor-class tools let professionals move like teams. Lovable-class platforms put development power into non-developers' hands. Both belong in a modern enterprise. The difference is placement and proof. Put each on the right tier. Give each the right human, make them accountable for the AI they oversee, and empower them. Demand evidence, not an AI narrative. Then let velocity compound—safely.

That's the promise of the accountability layer: rethinking your human workforce around a quiet discipline that turns "move fast" from a slogan into a repeatable habit of working with AI and moving on from generation tasks that compete with AI to new value-added ones of verification and realignment. We need to stop thinking of humans as something that slows the machine down, because the right humans, with the right gates, still make it possible to move much faster than we used to— but without bracing for impact.

CHAPTER TEN

Shadow AI & Vibe Coded Applications

By now, trust has been mapped in principle and tested under strain. What remains is to see how it behaves in motion. This chapter steps inside the workflow itself—the point where good intentions meet real automation. Here, we watch how "Shadow AI" takes root: how a quick prompt becomes a team script, then a quiet dependency. It's the turning point from theory to production, and from human oversight to system behavior. To make that leap safely, the work has to move along rails—predictable tracks that keep automation from veering off course. These rails aren't exclusively software features; they're the rules, constraints, and checkpoints that let innovation run fast without running wild - like the railway for a train.

When the Prototype Becomes the System

I've watched a weekend demo become a system of record. A teammate mocked up a screen to prove a point – a few buttons, a prompt, some connectors. By the following Monday, people were relying on it. Nobody owned it. Nothing was logged. When it misbehaved and caused a critical error, the room went quiet. Even the person who "built" it couldn't explain how it worked – most of it had been generated by a model. The issue wasn't speed or intent. It was business dependence without visibility.

Shadow IT used to wave red flags we recognized – a rogue SaaS purchased on a corporate card, an Excel macro only one analyst could run. Shadow AI arrives in friendlier clothes: a chatbot that drafts refunds, a quick workflow that posts customer notices, a thin UI written instantly by AI that looks official because it carries a team logo and feels polished. The problem isn't speed; it's that people shift where they anchor trust — the trust that underpins the business — without realizing it. Left resting on a model, we get activity without accountability: plenty of logs, little understanding of why we can trust the new way of doing things. Anchored properly in guardrails, evidence, and named humans, the same speed becomes tractable. And while speed helps the business, unmanaged speed widens the blast radius. We don't need to slow people down; we need to move trust out of the black box and into systems and roles that can take accountability for the work.

This chapter extends that same accountability layer into the world of *vibe-coded* apps — software assembled by non-developers using natural language and drag-and-drop logic, often with AI quietly doing the heavy lifting. It's the next evolution of shadow systems: not malicious, just invisible to the controls that once kept trust anchored. But the real challenge isn't any single tool or workflow — it's the production line itself. We've entered a world where anyone can spin up a micro-system that touches customers, data, and brand. Here, we focus on how to secure that creative pipeline: to make the work observable, ownership explicit, and verification cheap enough to scale. The goal is simple — preserve the creative speed that makes these systems valuable, while ensuring the enterprise can trust not just the code it didn't write, but the process that keeps producing more of it.

What "Vibe Coding" Actually is

Vibe coding shouldn't be a slur. It's shorthand for how people now build — where a domain expert can describe a task in plain language and get a working interface in minutes. They understand the work and the outcome; they may not understand the generated code. That's not negligence; it's a structural gap in the emerging software production line. And the risk isn't in the experimentation; it's when we create unexamined dependence.

Developers often bristle at this term, and for good reason. Done badly, vibe coding produces brittle, undocumented tools that can't be maintained or trusted. But done well, it unlocks a level of iteration and alignment that traditional development cycles simply can't match. It lets experts automate their own workflows while engineers focus on the guardrails, connectors, and shared services that make that freedom safe. In other words, vibe coding isn't a rebellion against software discipline — it's what happens when the business side finally gets access to the same leverage developers have always had.

Over the past year, I've found three truths consistently hold when people start building this way:

Truth	Why it Matters
Natural language is a powerful programming interface — but a terrible system of record.	People can usually describe what they want, but not why or how you can trust it later. Left unguided, we lose the replicability, auditability, and accountability we expect as standard from software when the code in question is compiled by an AI from natural language instructions.
Generated code can be correct and still opaque.	The model might produce flawless results that no one can explain or modify. Even if it works reliably, without someone understanding what is happening under the hood and taking accountability for it, any unverified output isn't something you can trust or scale.
People will depend on anything that reliably saves them time.	Once a shortcut solves a problem, it becomes production. Policy always lags behind convenience, so governance must start at the moment dependence begins.

If those points hold — and in practice my experience finds they do — banning vibe coding isn't a defense against risk; it's either self-inflicted blindness to Shadow AI or a competitive disadvantage created by denying non-developers access to the most powerful leveler for software production we've ever seen. The proper answer is to build a system of controls that make that speed observable, repeatable, and accountable — guardrails that are engineered and maintained by technical experts so the rest of the business can embrace vibe coding safely at full speed.

Converting Shadow AI from Risk Nightmare to AI Production Line

Many organizations already have the functional pieces of an AI development stack that lets non-developers safely produce working software solutions to their problems — they just haven't applied the discipline that we've discussed throughout this book. In most cases, these pillars weren't designed together, and most enterprises haven't combined them as part of a single security and trust system. But they're now where the real AI work actually happens — where prompts turn into workflows, workflows turn into customer-facing actions, and lastly where language can turn into software. Understanding these three layers and governing how they interconnect in your enterprise is how Shadow AI's speed can be made honest and sustainable.

Here are the components you need to select and secure within your enterprise to turn your Shadow AI nightmare into a disciplined AI Production Line; they are likely familiar to you:

Pillars	Core Purpose	In Practice (Examples)	How It's Normally Used
An AI Prompt Workspace	The environment where people meet models. Prompts, retrieved context, and generated results become shared work once they influence others.	ChatGPT (Custom GPT Editor), Microsoft Copilot Studio, OpenWebUI	Captures low-level intent for individual AI actions. Turns prompt engineering iterations from a code practice into general, business auditable steps — a record of what is tasked to AI, by who, and why. Defines how AI decisions are shaped by non-engineers.
A Workflow Platform	Where durable logic lives. Fast AI-authored workflows become standardized, versioned, and policy-aware.	Tines, SOAR systems, Power Automate, Zapier, n8n	Converts AI tasks and other engineering supported software actions into reliable, business reviewable processes. Introduces typed actions, approvals, and observability so automation remains auditable without slowing iteration.
A Vibe Coding Platform	AI-assisted development environments where natural language produces functioning code or applications. These systems often create interfaces, integrations, or agents that run atop existing workflows and data.	Lovable, Cursor Agents, Replit Agents	Represents a new edge of software creation — where **non-developers** generate code without realizing they're developing. Engineers may use Cursor too, but we differentiate here as focusing on the portion of such tools that support non-technical users.

None of this is exotic. Many enterprises already have some of these components officially sanctioned – fewer have thought about them as parts of an interconnected single production line. The discipline for a true AI production line lives at the seams between them: where a prompt becomes a process and where a workflow becomes something a customer sees.

For leaders, the first task here is awareness and recognition. Somewhere in your organization, these layers probably already exist officially or unofficially and are solving problems – an AI workspace where people experiment, a workflow platform where people string actions together, and a vibe coding platform where people are compiling software from natural language. Knowing where they are being used, how, and by who is the first step to securing them.

The next sections break down each layer in turn: how it works as part of the larger whole, where the risks appear, and the questions leaders should be asking to keep speed honest in the AI Production Line without losing control.

The AI Workspace

When to stop treating your prompts like private mail.

This is where AI work begins on the production line: wherever people in your company meet models. An AI workspace is any environment that lets an employee use natural language to get work done by prompting a model. It might look like a chat window, a prompt editor, or a customized assistant inside a productivity suite. Whether it's ChatGPT, Copilot Studio, or an internal tool built on OpenWebUI, the pattern is the same: a human describes intent, the model generates an output, and something operational in your business happens next.

In the early days, these workspaces were treated like notebooks – private places to experiment. Today they've become the front door to real business processes. The moment a given model's output is found to be useful, it will be regularly shared, sent, and repeatedly used. We need to recognize this moment as where a private workspace tool becomes an emergent shared process. AI is no longer a private sandbox; it's a part of production - it just has humans copy and pasting from other systems into it in order to keep things moving.

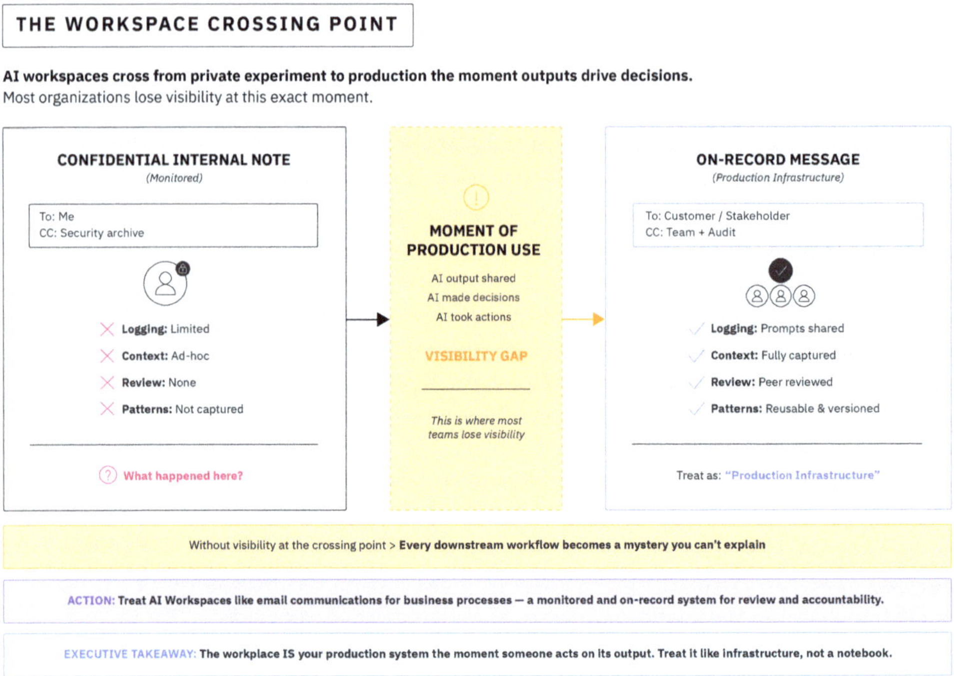

Chapter 10: Shadow AI & Vibe-Coded Apps — Layer 1: The AI Workplace

This shift is easy to miss, especially for security teams used to treating prompts as confidential communications — a sort of privileged conversation between an employee and a trusted digital assistant. But prompts aren't private messages; they're work instructions. They function less like an email to a colleague and more like the KB article defining a business process or a directive to an external subcontractor. When we treat them as secret rather than shared, we lose the context the business needs to understand what decisions are being made and why.

That transition — from private experiment to shared process — is where most organizations lose visibility. Once an AI workspace becomes a shared surface for action, it's the only system that records why the model produced what it did. The prompt is the instruction, the retrieval context is the evidence, and the result is the deliverable. If we lose visibility here, every downstream workflow becomes a mystery we can't explain after the fact.

The first task for leaders isn't to restrict these workspaces — it's to recognize where they already exist and how much of the enterprise's decision-making has quietly and organically moved into them. The goal is to make the intent of AI use at scale observable. Prompts, context, and outputs need to live in a shared environment where others can review and reuse them safely. This is where governance starts: not with a new policy, but with visibility into how, where, and why people are delegating the thinking, decisions, and actions of the business to AI assistants.

There are simple signals of maturity in this layer. Shared prompts instead of private ones. Persistent context that captures the data sources used. Logging that records what was asked and what was returned. These are the beginnings of accountability — a paper trail for thinking.

Promote a workspace pattern the moment you see the same prompt sequence reused daily by multiple people. When that happens, whoever is monitoring the prompts needs to recognize that it is time to promote that ad-hoc activity out of the AI Workspace to the next component - a Workflow. And, on promotion, the work runs on rails: inputs, tools, and side effects are gated and logged before anything crosses the decision perimeter. That's where AI involvement in our business logic becomes durable, versioned, and governed. But it starts here, in the conversational layer where human intent first meets machine execution.

This is where speed begins, and where trust is either captured or lost.

Promotion creates a boundary, but scale demands structure. Once multiple workflows exist, the question shifts from "what should this one do?" to "how do we control all of them?" That's where the platform comes in. Its job isn't to add more intelligence—it's to make sure every intelligent process runs on enforceable rails.

The Workflow Platform

By this point, prototypes are already in motion. The only way to keep speed without inviting chaos is to run the work on **rails**—predictable tracks that constrain inputs, tool access, and side effects. If a step leaves the rails, it stops. The boundary those outputs must cross to affect customers or systems is the **decision perimeter**. Everything that crosses it needs proof: who ran it, on what data, with what tools, and what changed.

Access to vibe coding platforms makes it tempting to wire prompt calls from the AI Workspace directly into production via traditional software. That path looks efficient until something breaks and there's no contract boundary the non-developers who produced the tool can inspect.

The definition of "non-developer task automation" rightly belongs on a **workflow platform** given clear ownership and support. You can buy it (n8n or an enterprise peer) or build it, but you cannot pretend that it maintains itself. A team of engineers owns the bricks and the runtime; but once the boundary is defined then business teams can safely own the logic they assemble from those bricks.

A serviceable automation platform has:

Capability	Minimum bar	Why it matters
Versioned blocks	Named, versioned actions with change notes	Enables rollback and reasoning
Typed connectors	Inputs/outputs validated and documented	Protects downstream systems
Sandbox runs	Fixtures and test environments	Catches surprises before they matter
Policy gates	Role/risk/data-scope checks at execution	Keeps speed inside bounds
Observability	Step-level logs tied to prompts and outputs	Builds the end-to-end story

Capability	Minimum bar	Why it matters
SLOs	Uptime/latency/error budgets	Treats the rail like a product, not a script pile. By rail I mean an enforceable track for automation: it constrains inputs, tool access, and side effects, and stops execution if a step leaves the track.

Buy vs. build is a time-to-safety decision. Buy when a platform gives you enforceable rails and visibility at the decision perimeter faster than you can staff it. Build when automation is core to differentiation and you own the people to maintain the rails. Either way, Layer 2 is where speed becomes explainable; put automations on a rail you can support.

The Vibe Coding Platform

What these platforms allow people to do is simple and powerful: express a business outcome in plain language and get a working interface almost instantly that appears to deliver it. A sales leader asks for pipeline heat and gets a sortable board with drilldowns. Operations asks for "exceptions in the last 24 hours" and gets a table with buttons that fire off actions. Legal asks for a "policy gap view" and gets a checklist linked to source passages. None of it requires an Integrated Development Environment (IDE). The platform infers structure from language, wires tools to data, sketches a layout, and remembers just enough of yesterday's context to feel coherent today.

Because they compress intent into interface, vibe-coded tools are extraordinary for discovery. They let non-engineers explore the shape of an idea quickly—not as a document or a ticket, but as something you can click. In the past, this level of validation required a sprint and a sympathetic developer. Now it takes an hour and a few prompts.

You'll recognize these systems by what they enable and how brittle they are once you look under the hood. The thing works—until someone else runs it from a different context, or the model adds a small update and breaks everything, or you find buttons that go nowhere and do nothing. When you see an impressive demo that no one can run twice the same way without the original author in the room, you might be looking at a vibe-coded system.

Used wrong, the pitfalls of vibe coding are predictable:

Risk	What It Looks Like in Practice
Unstable logic	The system appears consistent but radically changes behavior as new requests come in for updates – decisions can't be replayed or defended.
Hidden wiring	Behind every demo sits improvised connections between tools and data — no documentation, no review, and no single map of what depends on what. No one knows how it works. No one can describe exactly what is happening when a button is hit.
No accountable owner	Vibe-coded apps often run from a hosted account; when the person that built them moves on, the logic and history of the tool disappear with them.
Uncontrolled access	Early prototypes run with personal credentials or broad tokens, exposing sensitive systems to untracked, over-privileged use.
False finish	A polished interface creates the illusion of a deployed capability, when it's really a prototype that can't survive change or audit.

None of this makes the layer a mistake. It makes it a **design surface**. In isolation, that is its legitimate purpose. Treat vibe-coded apps as you would a high-fidelity Figma: a fast, shared way to converge on what good looks like—data in view where judgment is made, the right controls at the right step, the right evidence under the cursor. Judge them on clarity, not durability; on whether the interaction makes sense, not whether the result will hold when conditions change. If a team can't make the case on this surface, there's no reason to invest further. If they can, you've earned the right to turn that shape into something the enterprise can stand behind.

Examples make this concrete. A revenue team prototypes a renewal-risk cockpit that surfaces verifiable signals next to each account note. A security-operations lead mocks up a "human-in-the-loop" triage panel that shows the model's recommendation and the sources it relied on, with an explicit approve/escalate path. A policy owner drafts a rules explorer that lets auditors click from a control to the underlying evidence. In each case, the vibe-coded tool proves the interface and the information architecture. It lets stakeholders argue about what should be visible and when—without burning engineering cycles. That's the victory here: alignment at human speed.

Resist the urge to treat raw vibe coding platform outputs as software. From a trust perspective, these creations haven't earned that name. They're working drafts—valuable precisely because they are easy to change, and totally unfit to power anything that matters. When teams start relying on them for production decisions, the symptoms show up quickly: unexplainable divergence after a harmless update; policy logic that moved because a sentence did; outcomes no one can replay with the same evidence. That's what happens when you mistake a prop for reality – it looks perfect right up until you hit it like Wile E. Coyote and realize the tunnel you were aiming for was only painted on the wall.

Assembling the AI Production Line

Once individual rails exist, the next step is linking them into a continuous path—a production line for AI work. It looks familiar to software engineers, but the sequence changes once prompts and data share the same pipeline.

When you step back from the layers, their interdependence becomes obvious. The Vibe Coding Platform provides **expression**—a way for people to sketch how work should look and feel. The Workflow Platform provides **execution**—repeatable motion that can be verified and audited. The AI Workspace provides **reasoning**—the prompts, models, and evidence that guide intelligent behavior. But none of them can stand alone. Each layer protects a different dimension of trust, and without a shared frame to hold them together, that trust scatters.

What the enterprise still lacks—and what the industry is now learning to build—is the **scaffold** that joins them: a connective layer that turns experiments into systems of record. It binds creative design to accountable execution, linking every model call, workflow, and human decision into a single traceable chain. The scaffold supplies the rails across layers, so behavior stays within bounds as prototypes harden into systems. In a world where logic can rewrite itself overnight, the scaffold becomes the enterprise's memory—proof that what ran yesterday can be understood tomorrow.

HOW AI CHANGES THE PRODUCTION LINE

Traditional development is linear and gated; AI work only becomes sage when scaffolded rails add visibility and control.

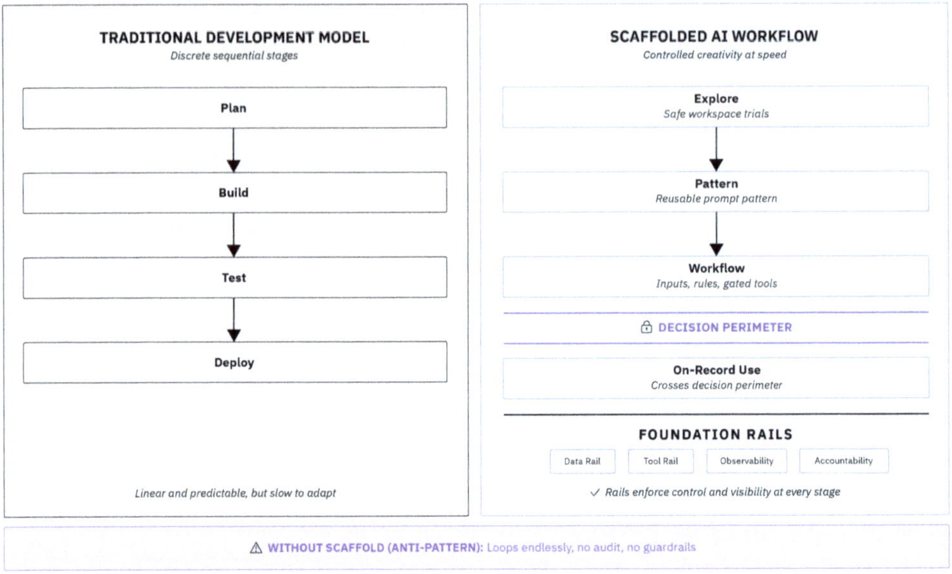

AI work becomes safe only when it runs on rails—patterns turn into workflows, cross the decision perimeter, and stay accountable.

Chapter 10: Shadow AI & Vibe-Coded Apps — Assembling the AI Production Line

Read the figure above left to right: each step builds toward on-record use, where rails validate data, gate tools, and make every action visible at the decision perimeter.

The rails shown above aren't abstractions—they're the structural logic of a trustworthy AI workflow. Each one converts what would otherwise be a fragile prompt into a governed process: data is validated, tools are gated, outcomes are logged, and the decision perimeter becomes enforceable. What follows unpacks that scaffold layer by layer, showing how those rails form the minimum viable infrastructure for safe automation.

This connecting layer doesn't yet exist as a single product, but we can already see its contours. It needs to do three things exceptionally well:

System Requirement	Purpose and Function
Translate design intent into governed plans	Natural-language prototypes from the Vibe Coding Platform become executable only after being formalized as **manifests** — structured documents that define required tools, data, and workflows. These manifests must be machine-readable for integration and human-readable for review, serving as living contracts: editable during design, versioned upon promotion, and authoritative for what the system can do.
Expose explicit boundaries between AI reasoning and operational action	When a vibe-coded app calls an AI function, it does so through the **AI Workspace**, where prompts, context, and model selection are logged and reviewable. Any resulting business action flows through the **Workflow Platform**, which applies role-based permissions, policy checks, and human approval gates. The connective layer orchestrates these calls so the AI can propose or decide — but can never act outside its governed perimeter.
Preserve traceability across creative and operational states	Every stage — from first prototype to deployed workflow — carries a single, end-to-end lineage: who designed it, who approved it, what models were involved, what data they touched, and which guardrails fired. This is more than compliance; it is the enterprise's **map of cognition and accountability**, proving how and why each outcome was trusted.

Taken together, these functions sketch out a control plane for intelligent work. I haven't seen a perfect implementation from a single product or vendor yet, but the direction is clear. The future enterprise stack to enable non-developers to operate an AI production line will need an orchestration layer that can lift ideas from the Vibe Coding Platform, refine atomic AI tasks in an AI Workspace, formalize chains of them in Workflows, and consistently return a result that's both explainable and safe to depend on.

Key Insight: The scaffold doesn't slow down the layers — it makes them safe to use at full speed. Builders stay creative; the enterprise stays in control.

Executive Takeaway: Most enterprises already have pieces of this stack deployed. The discipline lives at the seams — where prompts become processes, and where workflows become customer-facing code. The scaffold is what's missing, and what the industry is now building toward.

How Builders Actually Use It

Inside a properly assembled AI Production Line, building an AI app doesn't feel like compliance—it feels like working in a well-lit workshop. The same flows and tooling that once produced hidden wiring now produces visibility and repeatability by design.

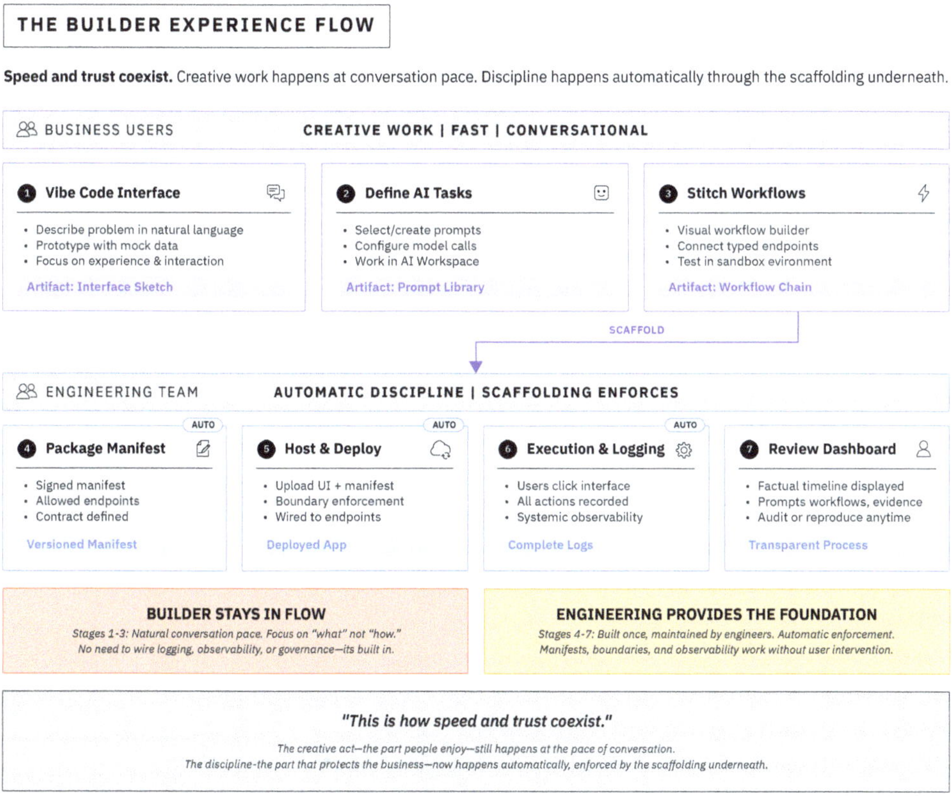

The experience starts with people describing their problem and vibe coding an interface. Builders can prototype in natural language using mock data and placeholders until the interaction feels right. The focus is on experience and problem definition, not execution—on getting the shape of the idea to make sense to real people. This is where the Vibe Coding Platform does its best work: fast design, human feedback, and visible alignment before any live data moves.

Once the design holds together, the builder defines or selects tasks for AI to execute in the AI workspace and then stitches them together visually in the Workflow Pattern. That package is the contract with reality: a bundle of approved endpoints that trigger inspectable work, resting on platforms engineers can support. Each endpoint is typed and described— exported as tools with clear input and output schemas—and wrapped in a signed manifest describing what the Vibe Coding Platform can hit when it goes live. This isn't a formality; it's the definition of what "safe to ship" means, and it allows the Vibe Coding Platform (with engineering platform support) to consistently produce functional software with user-inspectable logic.

Next comes hosting. The builder uploads the UI and its manifest to the host space. From that moment on, the app is only able to call what the manifest allows. The host automatically wires the front end to those sanctioned end-points—no custom glue code, no shadow integrations. The result is creativity with boundaries: the builder defines the experience, the platform and engineering teams define the perimeter, the AI writes the code for the interface.

Then comes execution and logging. As users click through the interface, the hosting environment silently records every back-end action: which MCP tool or model the app invoked, which workflow blocks executed, what inputs were passed, and what outputs came back. None of this depends on a developer remembering to log events— observability is systemic.

Finally, the builder opens a review dashboard. Instead of a model narrative or an unverifiable trace, the platform renders a factual timeline: prompts, work-flows, evidence, and results, all tied to versioned endpoints and manifests. Builders don't wire this review path; the host provides it automatically. What used to be "a working demo only its author understood" is suddenly a trans-parent process any reviewer can audit or reproduce.

This is how speed and trust coexist. The creative act—the part people enjoy—still happens at the pace of conversation. The discipline—the part that pro-tects the business—now happens automatically, enforced by the scaffolding underneath. The builder still gets to build; the enterprise finally gets to un-derstand what it built.

How Review Works in Practice

When someone presses a button, the platform captures: the current manifest, the model call (with retrieval context), the tool invocations, the workflow steps, policy gates, and the side effects.

Component	What it answers
Event timeline	What the user clicked and when
Model context	Prompt and retrieval set the model saw
MCP tools	Which tools were invoked with which typed inputs
Workflow steps	Which workflow platform blocks executed, with inputs/outputs
Policy gates	Which rules evaluated; pass/fail; who approved
State diffs	Before/after for touched records
Cost & latency	Tokens/compute by step; timing per leg
Anomalies	Injection flags, drift indicators, retries

When this is implemented well, builders can immediately see how their vibe coded UI invokes their defined AI model + workflows in real time, even though they don't know code. Security teams can audit to reveal risks, insert breakpoints, or require new guardrails as the app grows critical; and engineering can trace action level faults back to platform components with named owners.

How Review Works in Practice

A salesperson vibe-codes a small dashboard to help them stay organized in the field: it sorts leads, flags priority, and schedules follow-ups. The tool is successful; it's organically and quietly adopted across the sales organization.

Later, security notices score distributions drifting for a campaign. They add a breakpoint: runs with that pattern should require additional evidence. Engineering adjusts features in the scoring workflow. The seller keeps clicking the same button. The system shows its work, and the business retains trust in its sales process.

Review: Securing Your AI Production Line

Each control that follows is an echo of work we've already done. These aren't new doctrines; they're just the condensed lessons of the road behind us. When we said in Chapter 7 that trust must rest on something outside the model, the rules outlined in the table below are examples of that "something" made concrete.

When we mapped decision perimeters and risk tiers in Chapter 8, this is where those boundaries become enforceable form. When we framed accountability in Chapter 9 as a traceable chain between people and systems, these are the weld points that hold that chain together. Even the supply-chain cautions from Chapter 6 and the poisoned-prompt failures from Chapter 5 live underneath them—reminders that vigilance must now be structural, not episodic.

Taken together, the tables below are less a checklist than a distillation: the reflexes of a governed enterprise, where trust, evidence, and velocity can finally coexist.

Control	Practical Rule
Per-app identity	Each AI Production Line app has its own OAuth client/service identity; no shared tokens
Human-on-behalf-of	Actions run as the user with least privilege; audit trails bind both app and human
Allow-lists	Manifests restrict models/tools/workflows; platform enforces at runtime
Typed params	Tools and workflows validate inputs before side effects
Rate limits	Per-app and per-user throttles; circuit breakers on cost anomalies
Signed manifests	Changes require review; platform keeps history and diff
Sandboxes	Throwaways run in a fenced workspace; promotion flips to governed wrapper

Adding Validation Flows

Control rules alone don't secure a system; they steady it long enough for learning to take hold. The next step is securing the operational AI work – adding validation flows that keep those rules alive in practice. In deterministic software, we used tests to prove code behaved as expected; in AI systems, we must inject validation to prove behavior remains aligned as the world shifts around it. Every escalation, every review, every human check added to apps emerging off the AI production line become part of a living feedback loop – the same loop we first imagined back in Chapter 4, when we watched model behavior drift in the absence of oversight. Now, that vigilance is built in. The enterprise doesn't just react to failure anymore; it remembers, re-evaluates, and adjusts in real time before decisions turn to actions. This is what it means for trust to be operational – trust not just audited once; but something that's continuously renewed and attached to prove each output.

Validation Theme	How Our Scaffold Delivers it Systemically
Prompt injection & poisoned inputs	Build behavior baselines, trigger anomaly flags on the model-context panel; block risky workflows pre-validation
Retrieval drift	Compares retrieval manifests across runs; alert on shifts
Decision-risk tiers	Allows builders and security teams to require review ladders enforced per tool/workflow; sampling rates visible
"Cheaper than redo" review	Evidence panels let reviewers verify without re-creating work and track costs.

What the above table really shows is how risk tiering now lives inside the system, not beside it. Every validation flow already maps to a decision ladder – from quiet sampling in low-risk work to real-time human confirmation when stakes climb. We built those tiers back in Chapter 8 to decide who should be in the loop; now the scaffold lets us enforce them without breaking motion. The result is a rhythm that balances automation with judgment: lightweight review where confidence is high, deep inspection where impact is real. It's not new governance – it's governance remembering what it learned. Validation and risk have finally merged into the same circuit.

Adding Decision Risk and Review Ladders

Every modern enterprise experimenting with AI is already standing on the edge of this design problem. The pieces exist—review tiers, approval flows, risk scoring—but they live in separate tools and teams. What's missing is a shared rhythm that ties them together. Executives probably won't get that rhythm from a vendor anytime soon; it has to be built deliberately into the organization's operating model. The decision-risk and review ladders are how you decide what that discipline looks like in practice in your organization: proportional oversight that moves at the speed of automation without surrendering control. If you lead an AI initiative today, your real task isn't to slow innovation—it's to ensure every tier of risk in your AI production line has an accountable owner and a visible evidence path. Build that, and you're not just experimenting with AI—you're shaping the system that will let your business trust it at scale.

Risk Tier	Example Actions	Required control	Evidence to Surface
Low	Draft an email; summarize case notes; file an internal ticket	Post-facto sampling (e.g., 10–20%)	Prompt, retrieval sources, action summary
Medium	Update CRM fields; adjust entitlements; trigger refunds under threshold	In-app human confirmation	Before/after record + approver ID
High	Change policy; move money; broad customer comms; modify access	Dual approval + policy checks	Full trace + reversal path

Focus on Observability: Demand One Story from Prompt to Action

When something misbehaves, you want a single timeline: the prompt and retrieval context, the model output, the Model Context Protocol (MCP) tool invocations, the workflow steps, the approvals, and the downstream effects. That story shortens time to reason and time to repair. Here's what that can look like:

ONE STORY FROM PROMPT TO ACTION

Built-in observability with no manual instrumentation. Every action produces a single, traceable story that answers: what happened, why, who approved it, and what changed.

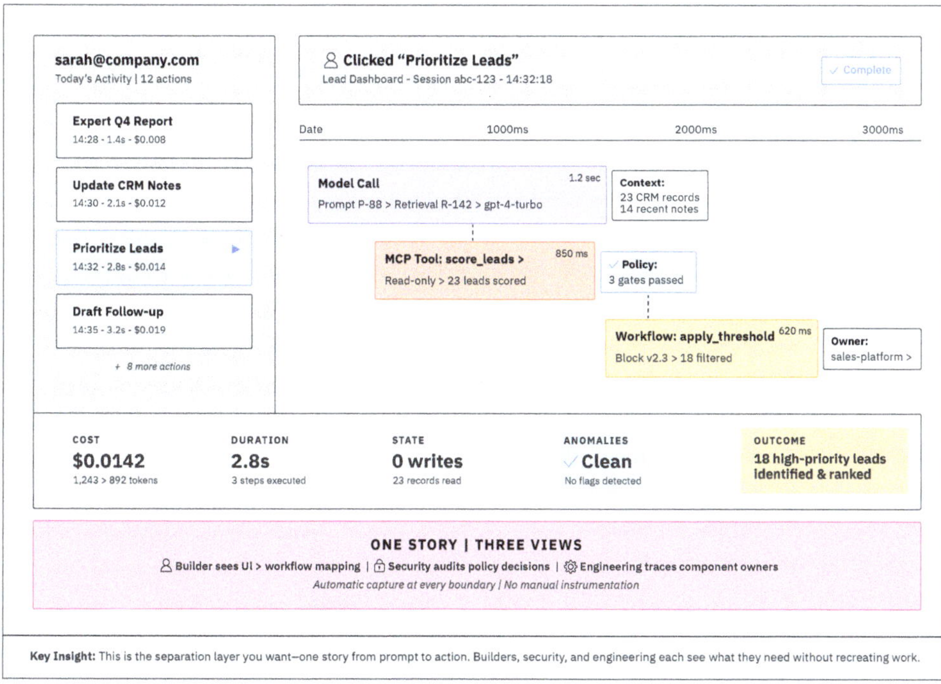

The AI Production Line isn't fully real yet, but it isn't just a concept on paper either. In my team's current lab work, we've already begun exploring early prototypes of the AI Production Line and the methodologies discussed in this book in practice. So far, we are testing small POC systems that connect prompts, workflows, and human oversight through shared evidence and policy gates. The results so far are promising: trust becomes visible, review becomes faster, and the work itself grows easier to reason about. These are still experiments, but they're experiments grounded in practice. We're still learning what holds up, what breaks, and what it really takes to make this architecture real. And as those lessons continue to unfold, I look forward to sharing more.

Conclusion

When I started writing this book, I thought it would be about AI. It turned out to be about leadership. About the responsibility that comes with seeing a technology change the boundaries of what people can do – and realizing that we get to choose how that change unfolds.

From the beginning, I said there were two truths we would have to hold at once: that AI is now essential to staying competitive, and that it introduces a new class of risks capable of utterly destroying the trust enterprises depend on. Those truths haven't changed. What has changed, at least for me, is how I see the work in front of us. The goal isn't to master the technology – it's to design the environment where it can be used responsibly, where speed and judgment can finally coexist.

We've spent these chapters tracing how that can happen. We examined how trust migrates – from people, to systems, to the structures that govern them – and how to keep that trust visible. We walked through attacks, guardrails, control planes, and validation loops, not because I think every executive needs to understand the mechanics, but because you can't lead what you can't picture. You have to be able to see what accountable AI work looks like before you can demand it.

And if there's one picture that stays with me, it's that of the future AI production line. A place where creativity, automation, and accountability move in rhythm – where the model is just one station in a longer flow. Some pieces are currently theoretical, yes, but the principles behind it aren't. We already know how to design for safety without suffocating innovation. We already know how to measure quality, and how to create evidence that travels with work instead of slowing it down. What's new is that we now need to apply those instincts and governance to reasoning itself – to the previously invisible but now essential work of thinking critically – before we can properly leverage AI-generated outputs.

That's the decision in front of us: to treat AI not as a clever assistant, but as part of the enterprise's memory and judgment. Because as models start making decisions, they aren't just executing logic; they're shaping how your organization evolves. The leaders who will succeed in this era are the ones who see such governance not as a tax on progress, but as the cost of confidence – who understand that verification isn't bureaucracy, it's emerging as value and brand protection.

I don't believe the future of work is about machines replacing people. I think it's about people learning to work through machines – to delegate without disappearing. Our task as leaders isn't to slow down innovation; it's to make it legible. To build systems that let us remember and audit why each decision was made, not just what the output was. To ensure that every act of AI automation leaves a trace of human intent behind it.

The companies that figure this out will move faster than anyone else, because they'll trust less blindly and be secure with their verifications. Their teams will be confident enough to experiment, and their customers will be able to stay confident in the results. That's what good governance really buys you: permission to move.

I've spent most of my career in security, trying to make sense of the ways technology breaks trust. Writing this, I realized that our job is no longer just to defend systems – it's to design them to be worthy of trust in the first place. We can't stop AI from changing how work gets done, but we can decide what kind of work emerges as the old work is made obsolete.

Glossary

Term	Definition
A/B Test	An experimental method that compares two versions of a system—Version A and Version B—to measure which performs better against a defined metric. Common in product design and AI workflows to evaluate prompts, model configurations, or interface changes before full deployment.
Backdoor	In cybersecurity, a backdoor is an intentional or hidden access point that bypasses normal authentication or security controls, allowing unauthorized users—often attackers—to enter a system, application, or network. Backdoors may be inserted maliciously or left unintentionally during development, creating significant security risks.
Digital Twin	A virtual replica of a physical object, system, or process that uses real-time data to mirror its real-world counterpart. It allows organizations to monitor, simulate, and optimize performance across a product's lifecycle.
Differential Privacy	A privacy method that adds mathematical "noise" to data so results can't reveal whether any individual's information was included. It enables useful analytics on sensitive data without exposing personal details.
Diff	In software development, a diff (short for "difference") shows what changed between two versions of code or files—what was added, removed, or modified. It's similar to "track changes" in a document and helps teams review, verify, and audit updates before merging them into shared systems.
Embedding Vectors	Numerical representations of data—such as words, images, or code—that capture their meaning and relationships. Used in AI systems to measure similarity and support semantic search and reasoning.
Integrated Development Environment (IDE)	A software application that provides a unified interface for writing, testing, and debugging code. In secure AI development, IDEs often integrate static analysis tools, dependency scanners, and code-signing workflows to detect vulnerabilities early and maintain model integrity.

Term	Definition
Mixture-of-Experts (MoE)	A neural-network design where multiple specialized "experts" handle different types of inputs. Only the most relevant experts activate for each task, improving scalability and efficiency.
Post-Processing of Responses	The refinement phase after an AI generates an output, where the result is filtered or adjusted for accuracy, tone, safety, or compliance before use.
Shepardizing	A legal research process used to verify whether a court case, statute, or regulation is still considered "good law." It involves checking subsequent citations in other cases using Shepard's Citations to see whether later courts have followed, limited, or overturned the precedent.
Sparsity	A design principle in which only a small portion of a model's parameters or neurons are active at once. It reduces computation, improves efficiency, and supports large-scale AI systems.
Static Analysis Scanners	Tools that inspect source code without running it to detect security flaws, bugs, or inefficiencies. They compare code structures against known rules to catch issues early in development.
STRIDE	A threat modeling framework used to identify common categories of security risks: Spoofing identity, Tampering with data, Repudiation, Information disclosure, Denial of service, and Elevation of privilege. It helps teams systematically evaluate potential attack vectors in system design.
Synthetic Content	Data such as text, images, or video created or modified by AI rather than directly captured from real-world events. Common in training models and generating new media.
Vector Databases	Specialized databases that store and search vector embeddings—numerical representations of meaning in text, images, or other data. They enable semantic search and retrieval in AI systems.
Zero-Shot Learning	An AI capability that allows a model to perform a task it wasn't explicitly trained on by applying general knowledge from other tasks or data.

Appendix: Quick Frameworks & Tools

AI Anti-patterns (and the Cures)

Every enterprise experimenting with AI eventually rediscovers these mistakes the hard way. This table is a field manual for early detection – the organizational "smells" that signal your production line is drifting from discipline into improvisation. Use it in design reviews and governance meetings to turn embarrassment into learning: it's not a list of sins, but a checklist for recovering trust before bad habits calcify.

Smell	What's Really Happening	Intervention
"We can't log our prompts – they're private"	Email metaphor blocking accountability	Draw the boundary: private for exploration; discoverable for app-invoked or production-adjacent calls
UI writes directly to a database	Short-term hack became a dependency	Move side effects behind platform workflows; export as MCP tools with typed inputs
Perma-pilot	No promotion path	Define a promotion checklist with dates; retire or wrap if it can't be promoted.
Plugin sprawl	Agents accumulate privileges quietly	Allow-list MCP tools; rotate/revoke unused exposure monthly
Shared admin accounts	Convenience over least privilege	Per-app identities; human-on-behalf-of semantics; audit trails
No owner for impactful actions	Responsibility avoided	Responsibility avoided

Review: Chapters 4–5 (Runtime and Threat Behavior), 7 (Anti-patterns and Trust), 8 (Control Pplane), 10 (Production-line Containment).

Promotion checklist (Pilot → Hosted Wrapper)

Innovation only scales when experiments know how to graduate. This checklist defines the minimum conditions for promoting a pilot into a governed service — when logging, manifests, typed workflows, and rollback paths are in place. Executives should treat it as the release gate between exploration and accountability: a lightweight control that keeps creativity moving without losing oversight.

Item	Done
Prompts and retrieval sources moved into the AI workspace with logging	
Workflow expressed on the rail using typed blocks and policy gates	
Layer 1/2 capabilities exported as MCP tools/resources where needed	
Platform-generated manifest carried by the app; signatures verified	
Pre-flights for medium/high-risk actions; evidence pane renders sources/gates	
Full trace available (prompt → MCP tool(s) → workflow → downstream effect)	
Rollback path documented (disable app, freeze prompts, block tools/workflows)	

Review: Chapters 3 Lifecycle of Experiments), 7 (Trust Pillars), 8 (Control Framework), 10 (Scaffold and Manifest)

Builder's Two-Minute Drill

Every engineer working with AI should be able to run this drill before shipping anything. It's the self-check that enforces the values of the book in two minutes flat: visibility, repeatability, ownership, and reversibility. Encourage teams to keep it pinned beside their IDEs — the fastest way to turn "trust as an engineered property" from philosophy into reflex.

Question	If "no," then...
Can someone else see what the model saw?	Move work into the AI workspace; capture retrievals
Can I run this twice and get the same steps?	Express it on the Workflow Platform with typed blocks
Do I know exactly what this button will do?	Add manifest-driven pre-flights bound to typed schemas
If it goes wrong, who can fix what?	Ensure endpoints are platform-owned; export workflows as tools and publish owners

Review: Chapters 7 (Transparency and Alignment), 8 (Human Workbench and Policy Gates), 10 (Converting Shadow AI to AI Production Line)

Metrics that Tell You Trust is Working

These are the leading indicators of maturity for an intelligent enterprise. They translate cultural health into numbers — speed, safety, cost, and resilience all reframed through the economics of verification. Use them in quarterly reviews or board updates to prove that guardrails aren't slowing delivery; they're making it sustainable.

Category	Metric	Why it helps
Speed	Time from idea → governed deployment	Confirms rails are enabling delivery
Adoption	% of automations on the rail vs. off	Reveals shadow-to-supported ratio
Safety	% of high-risk actions with dual approval	Tracks discipline where it counts
Quality	Reviewer rework rate	If reviewers must redo work, evidence is weak
Cost	Compute per successful outcome	Focuses teams on efficiency, not vanity usage
Resilience	MTTR for AI-related incidents	Responsib Tests whether one story really exists

Review: Chapters 7 (economics of trust), 8 (observability and audit), 9 (measuring human roles), 10 (traceability across layers)

Useful Signals for Validation & Risk Review Tools

The production line can only learn from what it can see. This table maps the raw signals that reveal drift, injection, waste, and human judgment gaps before they become incidents. Treat it as the instrumentation blueprint for your AI control plane: the sensory system that lets governance move at the same pace as experimentation.

Signal	Example	Use
Drift indicators	Refund rate for "polite" tickets jumps 30%	Surfaces behavioral change early
Injection flags	Odd Unicode or jailbreak patterns in prompts	Blocks obvious prompt-injection paths
Cost watch	kens per request and total compute per app	Catches denial-of-wallet and waste
Tool map	Which apps call which MCP tools and how often	Finds privilege creep and unused exposure
Human feedback	One-click to say "looks wrong" on output traces	Captures human perception as data—flags questionable reasoning, builds a corpus for retraining, and measures trust alignment over time

Review: Chapters 4–5 (drift and runtime threats), 8 (telemetry and guardrail design), 10 (validation flows and decision ladders)

On AI and Authorship

This book was not just written about artificial intelligence — it was also written using it as a tool.

AI has been part of my writing process from the very beginning, though never without a human hand on the wheel. In drafting this book, I used AI as a research partner, prompting it to surface and organize relevant raw material for each chapter. The goal wasn't to have AI "do the thinking" for me, but to accelerate the gathering of credible sources, examples, and perspectives I could evaluate, refine, and integrate. Every cited fact, every illustrative case study, has been reviewed and vetted by me — ensuring that the information came from appropriate sources and fit the real-world context of my professional experience.

When it came to shaping the chapters, the AI became for me a kind of creative co-collaborator. I used it to brainstorm structures, generate dozens of possible outlines, and explore alternative flows for this book as a whole. This helped me see options and perspectives I might have missed and to test different narrative arcs before committing to a final path. It was also my editorial sounding board — a tool I could consult to stress-test ideas, reorganize sections, and experiment with tone.

Once the drafts began to take shape, I combined the vetted research with my own original writing and years of prior work, then used a custom "ghostwriter" agent to help adapt rough language into something that more closely reflected my natural style. Even then, I reviewed every line, editing the output for clarity, accuracy, and voice until it met my standards. AI sped up this process considerably, but the accountability for what appears here rests entirely with me.

This mirrors the advice I'm giving to business leaders throughout the book: AI can handle much of your heavy lifting — the drafting, the analysis, the first pass at organization — but it should never be left to run unchecked and unreviewed. The human in the loop is what ensures relevance, truth, and trustworthiness. My role as an author here has been to align and guide the AI toward my goals, make the judgment calls it cannot, heavily edit its work, and take ownership of the final product.

The process you see here is not theoretical; it is exactly how I recommend AI be used in a business context — as a force multiplier, but never as a replacement for human judgment in any decision that carries risk for you.

I hope you enjoy reading this work as much as I enjoyed creating it.

www.ingramcontent.com/pod-product-compliance
Lightning Source LLC
LaVergne TN
LVHW050934210926
848482LV00013B/608
9781067345013